Anatomy of Denmark

ANATOMY OF DENMARK

Archaeology and History from
the Ice Age to the Present

Klavs Randsborg

Bristol Classical Press

This impression 2011
First published in 2009 by
Bristol Classical Press
an imprint of Bloomsbury Academic
Bloomsbury Publishing Plc
50 Bedford Square, London WC1B 3DP, UK
and
175 Fifth Avenue, New York, NY 10010, USA

A catalogue record for this book is available
from the British Library and the Library of Congress.

ISBN 978 0 7156 3842 2

Typeset by Ray Davies

www.bloomsburyacademic.com

Contents

Contents

Alvorlig taler ved alfarvej
med grønsvær tækket de gamles grave;
Henfarne slægter – forglem dem ej!
I arv de gav dig en ædel gave.

Solemn speaking at public highway
by greensward-roofed graves of the old;
Departed generations – do not forget them!
As heritage they gave you a noble gift.
Johannes V. Jensen, 1925

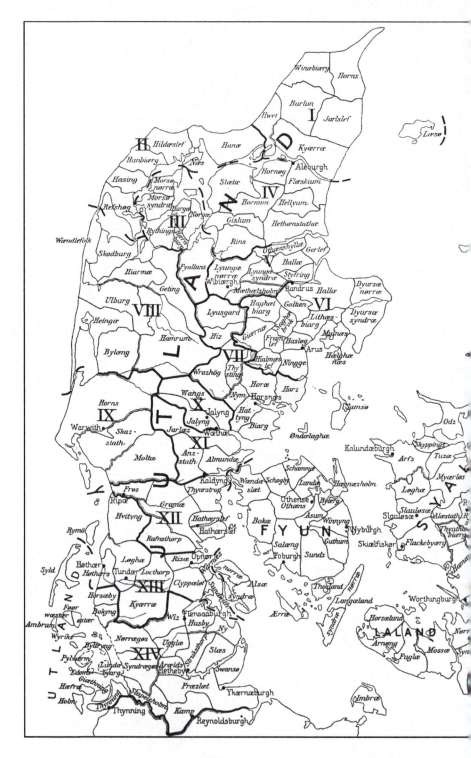

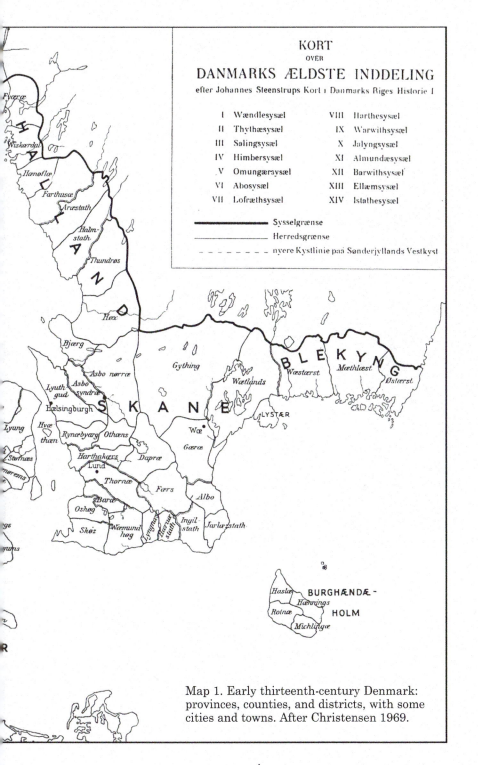

KORT
OVER
DANMARKS ÆLDSTE INDDELING
efter Johannes Steenstrups Kort i Danmarks Riges Historie I

I	Wændlesysæl	VIII	Harthesysæl
II	Thythæsysæl	IX	Warwithsysæl
III	Salingsysæl	X	Jalyngsysæl
IV	Himbersysæl	XI	Almundæsysæl
V	Omungærsysæl	XII	Barwithsysæl
VI	Abosysæl	XIII	Ellæmsysæl
VII	Lofræthsysæl	XIV	Istathesysæl

—————————— Sysselgrænse
————————— Herredsgrænse
– – – – – – – nyere Kystlinie paa Sønderjyllands Vestkyst

Map 1. Early thirteenth-century Denmark: provinces, counties, and districts, with some cities and towns. After Christensen 1969.

ix

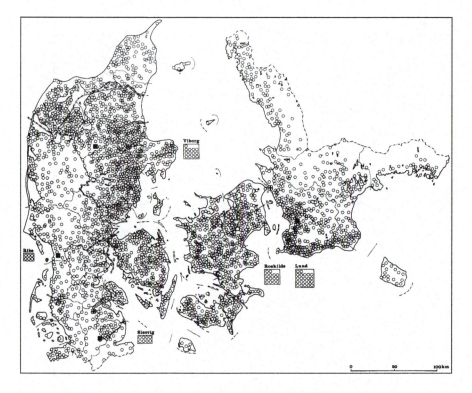

Map 2. Old Denmark, showing cities (squares) and medieval parish churches (circles). Nearly all the churches were founded in the Romanesque high medieval period. After Wienberg 1993.

Preface

For the times they are a-changin'
Bob Dylan, 1964

This is a small volume on a major theme: the archaeology and history of Denmark. I hope that it will be particularly useful to foreign readers. For the benefit of all, it presents the country's development from a specific perspective, centred on archaeology and the man-made material world. This is not to deny the usefulness and appeal of texts and other data; the aim is to emphasize a specific perspective often overlooked in general histories based on the written word.

An unusual feature is the deliberate emphasis on earlier periods, both in Part I which covers the distant archaeological past up to the High Middle Ages, coinciding with the emergence of historical Denmark, and in Part II which is concerned with the recent material past up to the year 2000. All major phases since the Ice Age – fifteen in all – are given more or less the same amount of attention, although more space is devoted to the later phases in order to include written information (see Table 1 on p. 147). The stress is on the specifically 'Danish' rather than on the generically European. Thus little space is devoted to steam engines or women's liberation, for instance, despite their importance. Part III contains additional information in the form of short topic essays and tables.

This approach may give the book a 'patchwork' appearance, perhaps more akin to history itself as it is experienced. The lavish use of figures and tables, together with 'windows' on selected themes, helps to heighten this effect. The material world is visual and often easier to explain and comprehend through figures than words. Readers should nonetheless find both presentation and argument to be coherent. The ambition is to be general while simultaneously building on personal studies and experiences.

England, parts of Scotland and Normandy, temporarily dominated by the Danes (or other Norsemen) during the Viking Age, are of course omitted from this account, as are other parts of Scandinavia, northern Germany and other regions which may have come under short- or long-term Danish rule. The area covered is so-called 'Old Denmark', including the eastern provinces lost to Sweden in the seventeenth century (see

Maps 1-2). The latter areas play a minor role in the discussion of the last couple of centuries. Local place names are used. Readers will find a moderately detailed map of Denmark and northern Europe of help. It is hoped that the few specialist terms employed are self-explanatory.

The present is a strange world. Over the past fifty years, the rapid increase of information has surpassed anything previously experienced. Nevertheless, the loss of history is immense, the past has been reduced to a form of entertainment and is rarely taught as a coherent story. Conflicts have arisen between globalization and tradition. Perhaps an understanding of the workings of history may help to fill this gap. This in any case explains this old-fashioned endeavour, to write comprehensively on a small region in a global age, rather than writing globally on a minor issue, as has become the norm.

I am grateful to my long-time friend, Professor Richard Hodges, for recommending this volume to Duckworth, and to Duckworth for its interest and support. My own institution, Københavns Universitet, has generously provided means for linguistic assistance, provided by Dr Erika Louisa Milburn, Rome.

The volume is dedicated to a fellow archaeological traveller, Dr Inga Merkyte, of the old Europe and the new world.

Part I

Archaeology: Ice Age to 1200 AD

... auk tani [karði] kristna
... and made the Danes Christian
　　　King Harald, on rune stone at Jelling, 960s AD

Introduction

Had this volume been organized along an equally subdivided time-line, only the final chapter would have been devoted to the last millennium (see Table 1 on p. 147). In other words, the centuries for which written sources on Denmark are available would have made up just a few pages of the entire work. All the other chapters would have been based on material history – on archaeological finds, studies and conclusions. However, while it is certainly possible to write an 'archaeological' history of all periods and even to perceive our own times through an 'archaeological lens', it is unwise to stop short at this. Rather, for all places and all periods we should draw on all available information, including, of course, written data. In fact, this is exactly what archaeology does when it engages with data on geology, geography, climate, vegetation, animals, indeed, on the whole environmental context of human actions – the greater stage of history. This stage became established long before the alphabet.

However, it would be a mistake to reduce archaeology to something akin to a modern social study of material culture, which merely acknowledges the emotional impact which objects, rooms, houses, spaces and so forth, as cultural idioms, have on human beings: in other words, to reduce the man-made material world to a science of recognition and effect, often applied to only a few select items or structures and not to the totality of human efforts, perceptions and actions, including their interplay with the natural world. There is thus no clear-cut dividing line between prehistory and history ('prehistory' was originally coined as a derogatory term by historians of written documents), nor even an oblique dividing line.

Defining Denmark
(see also below, p. 57)

'Denmark' can be perceived in various ways: the current state, the earlier states and the cultural areas still centred on the present kingdom (see Maps 1-2). The region's geography has changed dramatically since the Ice Age (Fig. I.1). Geographical contours similar to those of today, with Denmark lying between the North Sea and the Baltic Sea, and between the mountains, hills and forests of 'Norway' and 'Sweden' on the one hand, and the northern plains of 'Germany' and 'Poland' on the

3

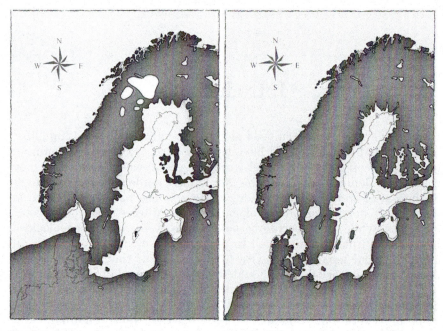

Fig. I.1. Denmark and neighbouring regions in different geological periods: (*left*) *c.* 7500 BC; (*right*) *c.* 4500 BC. After Andersson et al. 2004.

other, emerged only some seven or eight thousand years ago. Through the great river valleys, Denmark was ultimately linked with the eastern Mediterranean and the Near East, while other lines of communication were established with western Europe. There were fewer contacts (before the Middle Ages) with the eastern Baltic, possibly a reflection of differences not only in culture but also in language. Southern points of contact involved yet other cultures and languages, but in this case contact was in Denmark's greater interest, introducing domesticated species of animals and plants, metals and socially important information. Links with western Europe were sparce before the collapse of the Roman Empire in 500 AD, the most conspicuous early evidence of such contacts being the megalithic tombs of the Neolithic (late fourth millennium BC).

Archaeology

The most important science employed to investigate Denmark's distant past is archaeology, which also has a particularly long and fruitful tradition in the country. Danish territory was first inhabited by hunters and gatherers, but 4000 BC – an important caesura throughout Europe and the Near East – saw the introduction of agriculture. Indeed,

Denmark's later history can be viewed in the light of foreign impact on an unusually stable micro-region of Europe, with high population and production levels. Denmark is not sufficiently distant from hubs of cultural development – such as the Roman Empire – to be unaware of progress; yet it is far enough away to ensure more stable and slower development, in contrast to the dramatic vicissitudes of the Mediterranean. At the same time, Denmark lies at the 'handle' of the large Scandinavian 'Y'. These factors lie behind the emergence and survival of the later state of Denmark, as well as of its present-day society. With its core lands surrounded by the sea, Denmark even takes the shape of a moated castle.

Archaeology and related sciences give us a detailed understanding of the environment – and of environmental changes through the ages, of subsistence and settlement, economy and technology, clothing and taste, means of transport (including boats and fine ships), communications and trade, forms of social organization and political culture, weapons and warfare, cosmology and beliefs, burials and sense of place in the world: in short, the material history of Denmark up to the present.

To give but one example, the development of the Danish homestead can be traced, often century by century, from the Early Stone Age onwards, revealing family control over cattle and other crucial resources from the Neolithic and Bronze Ages up to the present day. A specific type of structure, the wide three-aisled longhouse farmstead – first appearing in around 1500 BC – actually has a history of over two and a half thousand years: a truly remarkable continuity at the household level which is unmatched in areas such as the Mediterranean.

Burials, indicative of relations between the dead and the living, represent another long archaeological sequence of cultural events and expressions, typically leading to discussions of gender, family, social stratification (differences in types and amounts of burial goods), political organization and so on. Yet graves are difficult to interpret. For instance, a richly equipped grave presupposes wealth, but is this equivalent to real wealth? Even more disconcerting: a poorly equipped grave does not necessarily indicate a poor person or a poor society. From the poor Danish graves of the Viking Age (eighth and ninth centuries AD) we could never have guessed the ability of these people to conquer England.

An extremely important set of archaeological finds are those relating to weaponry, battles and warfare. Danish society was heavily militarized in later prehistory and the Danish state of the late first millennium AD may even have been 'born in blood'. At any rate, development not only implies the use of natural and human resources but also a high degree of organization and constant adaptation to external and domestic changes and stimuli, the latter deriving not least from the south.

The movements of populations – and thus of different cultural and linguistic groups – are old questions in archaeology and are often very difficult to answer. It is safe to say that, on the whole, archaeology does not provide a cultural parallel to the well-known linguistic tree showing the development of languages. Rather, divergence and to some extent convergence are the cultural norms, reflecting constant communication. The problem of the spread of the Indo-European languages, for instance, cannot be resolved by seeking the *Urheimat*, or original home, of an archaeologically dominant culture.

In recent years, among the many natural and biological analytical techniques employed in archaeology, DNA and in particular the cheaper stable isotope analyses indicate closer relations between human groups and more frequent population movements than usually suggested by archaeology; studies of the human genome are also becoming extremely important. For instance, a recent study suggests that as many as 51 of the 82 human beings studied from the mid-third millennium BC in Central Europe died in an environment other than that in which they spent their childhood (Price et al. 2004). Certainly, culture is a means of participation. In the case of Denmark, the exciting challenge is to compare biological and archaeological information on the prehistoric foundation of a country presenting a very high degree of continuity and relative stability.

At any rate, as the climate changed and new plant and animal life developed, a 'cultured' landscape evolved with its roots in the Early Stone Age; characteristically, this landscape became more open as time passed. Archaeology is not only a science of man but also of the human impact on nature and on other humans. In short, biological systems are heavily influenced by culture. Climate and humans are the two main agents in environmental change as seen from the archaeological standpoint.

Human accomplishments

Before venturing into Denmark, it is worth recalling the major accomplishments of world archaeology in order to place Denmark in its broader archaeological and historical context (Scarre 2005).

(1) The earliest piece of important evidence concerns the deep African roots of the human race. Some of our first ancestors, the so-called Australopithecines, emerged more than 4 million years ago and only disappeared 1 million years ago (bipedalism is as much as 6 million years old). Various *Homo* species (*Rudolfensis*, *Habilis* and *Ergaster*), all with larger brains and probably some form of language, emerged 2 million years ago; the last individuals died out around 1 million years ago. *Homo Heidelbergensis* evolved from *Homo Ergaster* and disappeared only 250,000 years ago. *Homo Erectus*, common in Asia,

emerged 1.5 million years ago from the same line. The very earliest *Homo Sapiens* appeared in Africa 130,000 years ago, descended from a branch of *Homo Heidelbergensis*. The Neanderthals – not found in Africa – emerged from another branch of *Homo Heidelbergensis* 200,000 years ago. The last classic Neanderthals died out 30,000 years ago, leaving the world stage and its peopling to *Homo Sapiens* by the Ice Age. However, the early emergence of *Homo Sapiens* was not accompanied by equally early advanced cultural behaviour. That is an acquired attribute.

(2) Crude stone tools seem to have been manufactured as much as 2.5 million years ago. The two-faced hand axes ('bifaces') of the so-called Lower Palaeolithic period, carefully manufactured from nodules, are 1.5 million years old; finer variants are more recent. In the Middle Palaeolithic, some 80,000 years ago, classic Neanderthals produced tools from flakes. In the Upper Palaeolithic, advanced stone tools were made from blades and supplemented with a series of bone and antler implements. In Europe, the Upper Palaeolithic arrived 'overnight' with *Homo Sapiens* groups who expelled the Neanderthals; the latter, despite their larger brains, were culturally underdeveloped. Interestingly, art, including the famous cave paintings, was also introduced by *Homo Sapiens*.

(3) Soon after the end of the Ice Age (accompanied by cooler and wetter climates further south), experiments in domestication began in various favourable niches across the globe. The first objects were plants, varying from region to region, followed by animals (the dog was domesticated by the Upper Palaeolithic). The earliest area to produce a so-called 'Neolithic package' was the Near East, possibly because this is the world region with the highest number of potential domesticates, including wheat and barley, sheep and goats in hilly areas, alongside cattle and pigs (Diamond 2005). Advanced societies also emerged very early in this area. By 7000 BC huge socially segmented villages like Çatal Höyük had appeared in Anatolia. By 6000 irrigation agriculture had began in Mesopotamia, with the foundation of temple complexes – the latter giving rise to administration and, after 4000 BC, to writing and social stratification, as in the city of Uruk. As mentioned, 4000 BC is an important dividing line. By 4000 even faraway Denmark, settled by hunters and gatherers after the Ice Age, had become a cultural reflection of developments in the Near East. Interestingly, Egypt, always used as the symbol of ancient civilizations, is only second to Mesopotamia.

(4) The emergence of domestication gave rise to primary 'civilizations' in a number of cultural theatres across the globe, some dependent on developments in Mesopotamia, like Egypt and Pakistan, others clearly independent. China's Bronze Age societies, based on rice farming, emerged in the second millennium BC, while the American civilizations are much later, the Olmec of Mexico being of the first millennium BC and the Maya slightly later; the Incas (and their predecessors) appeared at

about the same time. When these evidently human societies became known in Europe around 1500 AD, they changed our perceptions of the world. As civilizations based on Stone Age technologies, they still do.

(5) The development of modern archaeology has provided a detailed time-space matrix for world archaeology and history, stressing centre-periphery relations and analogies. The Upper Palaeolithic and Mesolithic hunters and gatherers are in fact still with us, for example at Thule and in the Kalahari Desert. The last Neolithic farmers still exist in the Pacific. Bronze Age societies (disregarding the specific technology) can still be found in Africa. The same is true of Iron Age and medieval forms of social organization. The traditional great empires may have disappeared, however, with the possible exception of China. Western capitalism dominates a globalized world with various traditional cultures still surviving, often appealing to religious rights as the final bastion.

In this check-list of what should be common knowledge everywhere, Denmark is but a small region, albeit one situated at one end of the Baghdad-København (Copenhagen) cultural highway: fairly marginal in Europe, but still strategically located. With the northern world on the rise, this geographical position will remain important.

Periodization

Archaeologists are extremely good at establishing long time-lines for various phenomena and at studying their conjunctions. They are also good at defining historical caesura or stages (cf. Randsborg 1990). In what follows I will employ both techniques. The emphasis lies on interesting archaeological finds or groups of finds, reflecting the fact that history is often presented as a series of smaller histories, much as we all perceive the world.

There are very few traces of human occupation in Denmark during the Ice Ages. Then, as the ice melted and plants and animals moved into Denmark, human groups followed. In the Early Stone Age (or Mesolithic), hunters and gatherers lived very comfortably in the even milder climate while the first steps were being taken towards the domestication of animals and plants, and even village life, in the Near East. The later Mesolithic in Denmark, ending around 4000 BC, is contemporary with the proto-states of the Near East and with Neolithic village life in southern Europe, where metals were already in use and symbolic communication had developed into a form of writing. Genuine alphabets, an administrative invention, were established by the mid-fourth millennium BC in Mesopotamia, on the threshold of the Near Eastern Bronze Age dynasties and their great monuments, such as the pyramids of Egypt (mid-third millennium BC).

As indicated, 4000 BC is more than just a convenient caesura. Beforehand we have simple agricultural societies in Europe, often linked to specific environments. Afterwards we see the expansion of societies with diversified economies, ploughs and subsequently wagons, wool for clothing and a wider use of metals. A new emphasis is placed on individuals, not least on the roles of males as the heads of families and as warriors. This development is connected with the more important role played by cattle.

There is a marked difference between developments in the Near East and in Europe. In Europe the entire continent was populated and was thus less specialized; in the Near East, development was concentrated in limited highly productive and densely populated regions such as Mesopotamia and Egypt, thus seeing the development of civilizations. In turn, these civilizations provided new stimuli for Europe.

In the following discussion of Denmark the stress is on contexts, relationships and changes – the ingredients of history. Professional

9

archaeology uses the same tools when establishing detailed chronologies and cultural relationships. However, archaeological details are not an end in themselves. The aim is rather to outline the cultural and social picture drawn by archaeology: leading up to medieval Denmark and thence to recent and present times. The following phases and terms are employed (Randsborg 1989):

Phase I: Hunters and Food Gatherers (in very different natural and cultural environments: from tundra to oak forest, from reindeer hunters to stable coastal adaptations; from the Ice Age to 4000 BC).

Phase II. Plant Growers and Herdsmen (the first Stone Age farmers, builders of megalithic monuments, villages of the ancestors, copper and prestige items; to the beginning of the third millennium BC).

Phase III. Cattle Breeders and Sun-Kings (differentiated Stone Age economies, individuality, daggers and swords, the rise of the international Bronze Age elites, sun-worship, hall-buildings, chariots and large paddling boats; to c. 1100 BC).

Phase IV. Farmers and Tribesmen (intensification of agriculture, introduction of iron, large rowing boats, establishment of large tribal units, impact of Mediterranean societies including Rome; to the third century BC).

Phase V. Courts and Armies (kingdoms of the Migration Period, the developed Nordic Pantheon, the post-Roman Germanic *koinê*; to c. AD 700).

Phase VI. Lords and Sea-Kings (rise of estates and mass production, sailing ships, international trading and raiding; Islamic connections; to the tenth century).

Phase VII. Kingdom Builders (the Jelling dynasty, Christianity and the Danish Empire (conquest of England), Byzantine connections; tenth to eleventh centuries AD).

Phase VIII. Christian Modernizers (Denmark becomes a European Christian kingdom; estates and church building, creation of modern settlements including villages and towns; to c. AD 1200).

Phase I. Hunters and Gatherers (to 4000 BC)

The Late Palaeolithic and Mesolithic periods in Denmark are characterized by a long series of extremely well-adapted cultures, mainly defined by their differing flint inventories and often with wide-ranging connections abroad (see Fig. I.1). First to arrive were the reindeer hunters of the tundra who initially even hunted mammoth. Later, with the appearance of different types of forest – birch and hazel, pine, and finally lime and oak (beech trees did not arrive until the Iron Age) – other animals such as elk, bear, even bison and wild horse, and certainly aurochs, red and roe deer and wild boar followed; many of

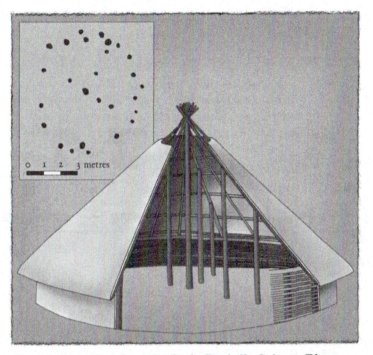

Fig. I.2. Round hut from the Early Ertebølle Culture: Tågerup, Skåne, with plan of post-holes. After Andersson et al. 2004.

these (such as wild horse, bison, bear and elk) no longer live in Denmark. These large animals were accompanied by numerous smaller species and, of course, valuable birds. In the sea, seals were always present. Fish were plentiful in the seas, lakes and rivers.

Excavated settlements have given their names to various cultural phases, including the Late Palaeolithic Hamburg Culture of the cold thirteenth millennium BC (when mammoth were still present). The Bromme and Federmesser Cultures (the latter named after a particular type of knife, the former after a site on Sjælland) of the twelfth and early eleventh millennium BC thrived in a warmer intermediate period with some forest. The later Ahrensburg Culture of the late eleventh and tenth millennium BC, named after a site near Hamburg, represents the last cold phase of the Ice Age, ending in 9500 BC. There are also a few traces of occupation during a warm phase about 100,000 years ago. The latter hunters were no doubt Neanderthals, whereas all other 'Danes' belong to the modern *Homo Sapiens* species.

The Mesolithic Maglemose Culture is named after a pine forest settlement on Sjælland of the ninth to mid-seventh millennium BC. These groups had counterparts living on the partially dry North Sea and in England, as well as in northern Germany and Poland. The

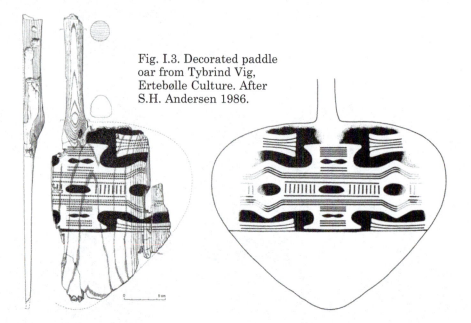

Fig. I.3. Decorated paddle
oar from Tybrind Vig,
Ertebølle Culture. After
S.H. Andersen 1986.

Kongemose Culture, also named after a Sjælland site, represents hunters and fishermen from the phase when Denmark began to take on its present form in around 6000 BC, during the so-called Atlantic period (7000-4000 BC).

The Ertebølle Culture dating from the mid-sixth millennium to shortly after 4000 BC is named after a famous kitchen or shell midden site in Jylland (Figs I.2-3). This culture is characterized by pronounced coastal adaptation, with the population exploiting a wide range of marine resources alongside terrestrial resources from the oak forest, obviously living in well-defined micro-regions and highly knowledgeable about all aspects of their environment. Their houses were family-sized and often fairly similar to those of the earliest food-producers (farmers) (Figs I.2; I.5). Graveyards near the settlements present a clear differentiation on the basis of gender and age, with women being buried in jewelled dresses (Albrethsen and Petersen 1976) (Fig. I.4). A newborn baby boy from Vedbæk on Sjælland, resting on a swan's wing by the side of a woman, is equipped with a flint knife. Another grave in the same site holds a man, a woman and a small child; the man was killed by the spear stuck in his throat, a grim reminder of conflict in societies often perceived as idyllic. At Skateholm in Skåne another important cemetery has individual burials of dogs (Larsson 1988).

The Mesolithic people of Denmark were short and heavily built with coarse facial features. They shared some features with today's Inuit, while others were typical of Neanderthals. Neolithic and later people

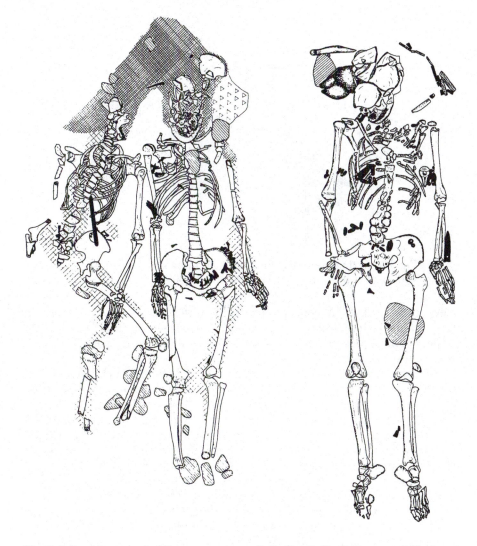

Fig. I.4. Double grave holding two women (*left*), Ertebølle Culture, and Early Neolithic male grave (*right*) from the same location at Dragsholm, Sjælland. The bones of the man, *c.* 20 years old, show a largely terrestrial diet, while those of the females, *c.* 20 and 40 years of age, show a marine diet: despite living in the same environment different choices were made by hunter-gatherers and agriculturalists (Price et al. 2007). On the basis of his weaponry the man was a hunter and warrior, which may explain why he is buried at the same strategic location as the Mesolithic women: between open coast and inlet. After Petersen 1974.

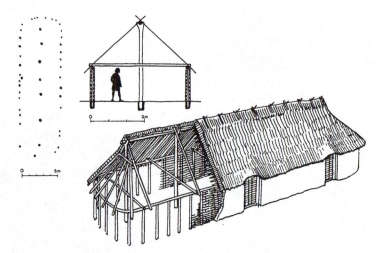

Fig. I.5. Early Neolithic farmstead from Limensgård, Bornholm, with plan of post-holes. After P.O. Nielsen 2001.

were taller (likely a consequence of a different diet). More gracile individuals – like today's population – emerged in the late fourth millennium, replacing their heavier predecessors: beauty-based natural selection perhaps.

We have a wealth of data on the Danish Mesolithic thanks to the fact that lake and riverside settlements have preserved large amounts of organic materials, from animal bones and antler implements to bows, music instruments, boats and even paddles beautifully decorated with patterns reminiscent of those of the North-West Coast Indians. The Danish kitchen middens of the Ertebølle Culture – refuse mounds containing shells, animal bones, flint and bone tools, and pottery – were the first prehistoric settlements ever investigated. They helped to give Denmark its central place on the archaeological world map, not least for the collaboration between various scientific fields. Ertebølle even gave its name to a widespread Late Mesolithic phenomenon characterized by fairly stable maritime communities using thick-walled pots with pointed bottoms to cook mixed meals of fish and meat.

A rather more classical achievement pertains to the realm of chronology, in which C.J. Thomsen's famous three-age system of Stone, Bronze and Iron Ages, demonstrated in his museum in København shortly after 1817, proved generally applicable to the Old World (Jakobsen 2007). A chronological system for Ice Age cultures was only established 50 years later, when Thomsen's system had already seen its first subdivisions and refinements both in Denmark and other European countries.

Phase II. Plant Growers and Herdsmen
(4000-3000 BC)

In Denmark, the cultural caesura of 4000 BC sees the introduction of agriculture and domesticated animals, even the plough (the simple ox-drawn *arð*), the use of flint mines to provide large pieces of high-quality stone for tools and other items, even copper (acquired directly from the Alps, perhaps on expeditions), battle axes as male symbols of power, flat-bottomed pottery (indicating the use of furniture) and so on. A ritual package includes monumental tombs, often in stone ('megaliths'), ritual 'villages' and the like. New population groups from south of the Baltic were probably involved in this complex and significant transformation.

Ritual sites, such as Sarup on south-western Fyn, were possibly meant to be homes for the spirits of the dead (N.N. Andersen 1997-99) (Fig. I.6). These particular sites are surrounded by palisades with several intricate entrances and long pits with deposited materials, including human bones and fine artefacts. The central areas, however, are virtually empty. Other, somewhat later, cultic structures comprise burned-down buildings filled with fine pottery. Decorated pottery is a central element in ritual performances, as is amber – thousands of beads were deposited – and very large and carefully polished flint axes, too long for normal use. The latter, like the copper axes, may be interpreted as elements in intricate exchange systems terminating with the deposition of these valuables in wetlands. Leadership must have been linked to knowledge and technological performance.

Megalithic tombs are spread across settled areas, where they create the earliest cultural landscape with clear imprints and reference points created by humans (see Topic 1: Jordehøj Passage Grave). The original number of these graves may have been as high as 40,000 on present-day Danish territory alone, each taking roughly 10,000 man-hours to build. Like their counterparts in western Europe, these tombs are truly impressive, whether they are dolmen chambers in stone settings sometimes over 100 m long or closed and elaborately constructed passage graves – the oldest surviving chambers in the world. Carbon-14 analysis of the birch bark used together with slabs to fill the spaces between the boulders has provided extremely accurate dates for the construction of the passage graves: 3350-3100 BC, while pottery may indicate an even narrower time-frame in the 33rd century BC for the 700 or so passage graves surviving in present-day Denmark (the original number was probably around 4,000) (Dehn and Hansen 2000). Varying layers of stone, earth and even flint in vertical 'channels' inside the mound served, along with the birch bark, to keep the passage graves dry and thus to preserve them.

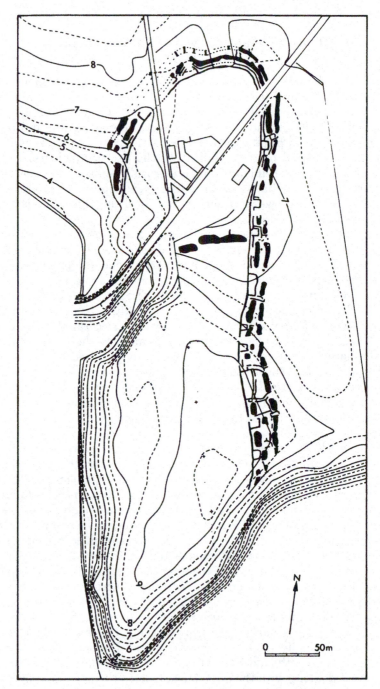

Fig. I.6. Early Neolithic ritual village, Sarup, Fyn. After P.O. Nielsen 2001.

These graves are highly innovative and time-consuming structures whose construction required considerable engineering knowledge, including the transportation and lifting of huge boulders. Their brief period of construction is reminiscent of the Egyptian pyramids more than half a millennium later. Perhaps a similar change in beliefs was taking place in both cases: spirits were no longer immortalized by placing the dead in *newly* built megalithic tombs (cf. Kaul 2004: 190f.). Some of the graves from the period after the construction of the megalithic tombs resemble ox-drawn carriages and are placed in kilometre-long lines issuing from old passage graves, as if participating in the travels of the spirits.

By 3000 BC this splendid 'Copper Age' was already in decline, perhaps because its dependence on fairly heavy soils where slash-and-burn forms of agriculture could be repeatedly practised narrowed economic decisions. More likely, perhaps, its heavy ideological, almost theocratic, superstructure could not be maintained, in much the same way that the slightly later Egyptian construction of pyramids came to an end.

Phase III. Cattle Breeders and Sun-Kings
(3000-1100 BC)

The second important caesura dates to shortly after 3000 BC, contemporary with the beginning of the Bronze Age in Greece and the Near East. Changes include an opening of the landscape and a large-scale use of ox-drawn wagons. The highly organized, even sophisticated 'megalithic' society collapsed, leaving a 'black hole' at its centre of gravity, Central Denmark. Nevertheless, the people of the megalithic were considered important ancestors and their monuments were used for burials until about 1500 BC, or the beginning of the Danish Bronze Age.

New identities developed, alongside diversified economies, including a return to hunting. Cultural links were wide-ranging, as exemplified by particular battle axes and ceramics, but new cultural boundaries also developed, even in Øresund: according to the pottery, no women from Skåne were married to men on Sjælland (supposing that the potters were women). By contrast, battle axes from Skåne belong to an artefact family stretching to as far away as the Urals. In Jylland, groups emerge who exploit marginal lands never hitherto tilled. This particular battle-axe culture has links to northern Germany and the Netherlands. Soon other groups become important, including some from western Europe, but the overall picture remains one of diversity, as exemplified by burial customs with graves in small mounds, simple stone cists and so forth.

By 2000 BC, when Greek Bronze Age palaces like Knossos on Crete were built, Central Europe and even Denmark were taking two important steps towards a Bronze Age proper. The first was the far more

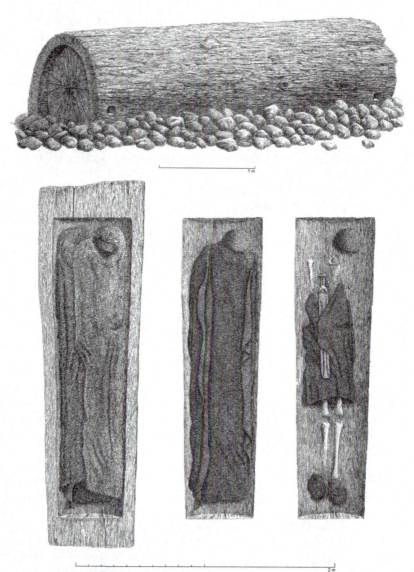

Fig. I.7. Muldbjerg man, Jylland, buried 1365 BC; (*opposite*) grave-goods from the burial. After Randsborg and Christensen 2006.

widespread use of metals – copper, tin and gold – which of necessity had to be acquired from abroad. Except for a few simple tools that could be cast in reusable moulds, all other bronze objects were made using the lost-wax method and are therefore unique. This implies that their shape and decoration (also cast) must have held a high degree of significance in terms of personal taste and choices, regional reference points and international cultural position. Typically, men's weapons often have an international aura about them whereas women's jewellery is more local in character.

The second step entailed social stratification and the development of an aristocracy, supported by alliances and cosmological or 'scientific' knowledge, as exemplified by the famous 'Sun Chariot' from Sjælland showing the course followed by the sun and the calendrical knowledge that this implied (Randsborg and Christensen 2006) (see Topic 3: Bronze

Fig. I.8. Young Skrydstrup woman of the late Early Bronze Age; (*below*) grave-goods (gold ear-rings and antler comb). After Randsborg and Christensen 2006.

Age Cosmology). The rise of the aristocracy also diminished regional differences. The elites present themselves in the famous oak-coffin graves within large mounds of the late second millennium BC, like the famous Egtved and Skrydstrup 'girls' (or rather princesses), the Muldbjerg man, and the 'royal family' from the huge Borum Eshøj burial mound – all resting on ox-hides (Figs I.7-8; see also cover). The organic materials have survived thanks to a special 'wet' technique, no doubt applied to preserve the bodily home of the spirit. These people lived in huge wooden longhouses (Fig. I.9), sometimes measuring more than 500 square metres, almost as large as the great hall of the Renaissance palace of Kronborg – Shakespeare's 'Hamlet's castle'.

The burial mounds were located along coastlines and roads as a testimony to the deeds of ancestors. In fact, a whole Early Bronze Age road network can be reconstructed on the basis of strings of mounds (Fig. I.10). This period also sees the introduction of light two-wheeled horse-drawn chariots, identical to those depicted in Bronze Age Greece

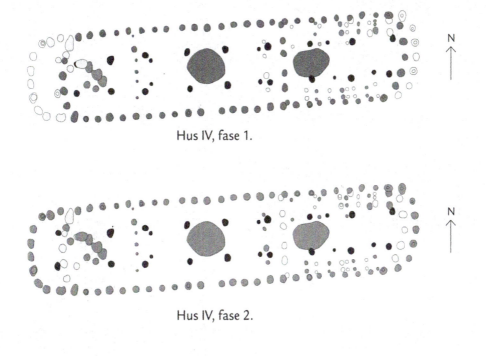

Hus IV, fase 1.

Hus IV, fase 2.

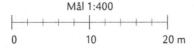

Mål 1:400

0   10   20 m

Fig. I.9. Early Bronze Age three-aisled longhouse farmhouse from Skrydstrup (Brdr. Gram), South Jylland. After Ethelberg et al. 2000.

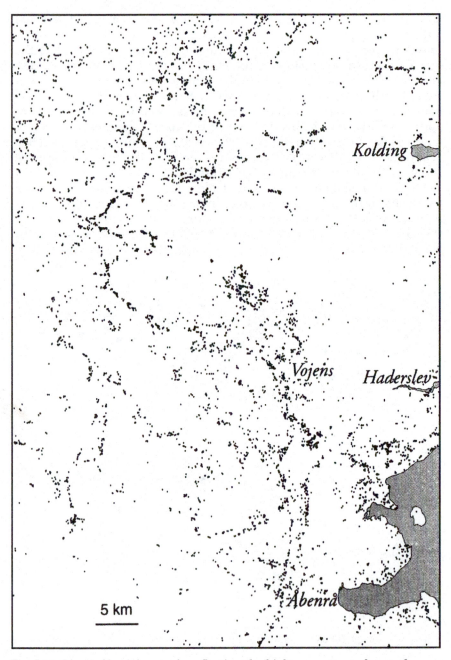

Fig. I.10. Lines of burial mounds reflecting the highway-system of part of Jylland in the Early Bronze Age. After Randsborg and Christensen 2006.

and found in Egypt, for instance in the tomb of Tutankhamun. Even the prestigious folding chairs used by Danish Bronze Age royalty are identical to Egyptian (and Greek) specimens.

A particularly significant monument is the huge cairn on the beach at Kivik in Skåne, measuring 75 metres across (Randsborg 1993) (see Topic 2: Kivik Grave). It holds a three-metre-long stone cist, excavated in 1748. On the eight stones of the long sides are rock-carvings, a feature normally found on natural rocks or large stones. The panels depict a whole Bronze Age 'university' in the form of cosmological symbols, mainly related to the sun, divine and royal insignia, aristocratic processions, and – probably – an interpretation of the levels of the universe.

The oak-coffin graves contain a complete set of woollen clothing for both men and women. The men wear a coat or loincloth and a large mantle; on their head they have either a soft pixie-cap or a thick helmet-like hat. The graves also contain blankets and leather shoes. A fur mantle and a skin cap from the bog-body found at Emmer-Erfscheidenveen in the Netherlands provide information on everyday outdoor garments (van der Sanden 1996: 76, Fig. 92; 148, Figs 205 and 191). The women all wear a sort of 'T-shirt' with sleeves to below the elbows and either a heavy string skirt, perhaps a cult dress, or a large square piece of cloth which may be worn in several ways. On their head they may have a bonnet, on their feet leather shoes. Blankets were probably used as additional garments. Neither women nor men wore underwear. The garments are simple and beautiful in appearance; finely woven belts and refined coiffures confirm this impression, as do the gold and bronze jewellery, including the sun-disc plates on the bellies of women, necklaces and bracelets. Like the famous sun-chariot, the belt-discs (and other cult items), contain in their various decorative elements important information about various calendrical systems (Topic 3: Bronze Age Cosmology).

The appearance of elite men in their fine mantles is as striking as that of the women and is enhanced by weaponry – bronze daggers, swords, weapon axes and so on – alongside gold bracelets and sticks for steering chariot horses. In addition, men carried razors, tweezers, strike-a-lights and other smaller artefacts with them in a purse; folding chairs – like small thrones – were also included.

The bronze and gold found in the graves make some statistical calculations possible (Randsborg and Christensen 2006: 23ff.). Generally, elite men possess far larger quantities of imported metals, in particular gold, than elite women. There are far more 'poor' than 'rich' graves. However, symbols of rank such as gold cluster in the 'bronze-rich' graves. As for the men, the top 20% possess half the bronze by weight, the top 25% as much as two thirds of the bronze by weight (and most of the gold). Translated into other resources, like cattle, land or forest, this is clearly a highly stratified society.

An unusual situation is found in north-western Jylland at the end of the Early Bronze Age, with very few poor male graves but numerous rich ones (swordsmen with gold bracelets). There are up to 50% more burials than normal as compared to agricultural resources and the graves cluster in two geographical groups. The region, rich in both soils and marine resources, nevertheless shows clear signs of over-exploitation. Probably population pressure led to the creation of a highly stratified double-kingdom, which collapsed in spite of close contacts with both south-western Norway and the west coast of Jylland.

The individual kingdoms of Early Bronze Age Denmark may have been quite small, roughly 1,000-2,500 square kilometres in area, but they were closely connected with one another in terms of culture. Although Sjælland played a special role, economic, social, cultural and religious homogeneity prevailed from the mouth of the Elbe River to north of the Trondheim Inlet in Norway, and from the island of Bornholm to Central Sweden (the northern regions of Scandinavia are different). We could even postulate a Bronze Age Union of '1397 BC' as a parallel to the Kalmar Union of AD 1397 between the Nordic countries. This is not to deny the existence of conflict, as demonstrated by the heavy weaponry and deliberate destruction of particular male graves: attempts to make some specific enemy spirits homeless (Randsborg 1998).

Phase IV. Farmers and Tribesmen
(1100 BC-250 AD)

Perhaps surprisingly in conventional archaeological terms, the next caesura should be placed in the middle of the Bronze Age, when farmsteads both diminished in size and became more numerous. The small oval fields of earlier periods were replaced by large rectangular ones. In the late first millennium BC scattered farms often clustered in hamlets, sometimes with a shared fence, as at Hodde in Jylland (Hvass 1985) (Fig. I.12).

Towards the end of the second millennium BC, new beliefs dictated the practice of cremation – as in the rest of Europe – and a diminishing use of grave goods. This is the period when Bronze Age society collapsed in Greece and the Near East; in Europe, a degree of continuity can be observed. That the old elites in Denmark were also being challenged seems clear from the farmsteads, while huge systems of fields and pasture indicate the rise of an organized landscape. A peculiar feature is the lavish depositions in the ground or in wetlands of gold bracelets, gold and bronze vessels, huge lur trumpets (in pairs), thin shields and so on, all instruments of cult and social display. Other deposits are more mundane, including weapons, tools and jewellery, and are often broken. Some archaeologists claim that all these finds represent forms of

24

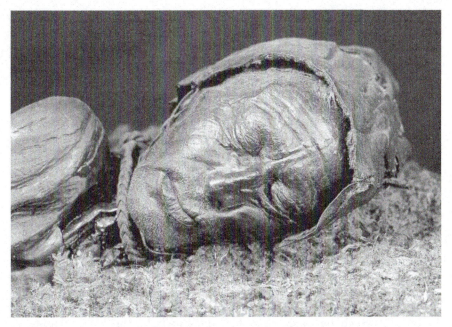

Fig. I.11. Tollund Man, Jylland; *c.* 400 BC. After van der Sanden 1996.

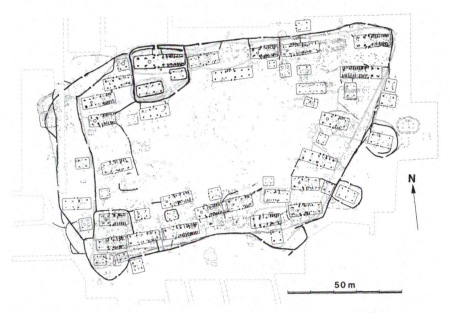

Fig. I.12. Hodde village, Jylland, first century BC. After Hvass 1985.

sacrifice, others that they are treasures. We could also interpret the fine ritual artefacts as deposited 'crown jewels', indicating the 'death' of a particular society. (The other deposits may be treasures.)

Iron is introduced in around 500 BC, dealing the final blow to the power of the remaining Bronze Age elites. In terms of settlement and agriculture, burials and so forth, no major changes took place. Large settlements emerged at around the time of the birth of Christ. Iron was produced locally in Denmark from the start of the Iron Age (it was known already in the Bronze Age), first in small pit-ovens and later in high-yield shaft ovens like those used in Africa until quite recently. High quality iron products, such as fine sword blades, were imported.

As indicated by the famous Hjortspring boat and weaponry deposit, battles were now fought by small homogeneous regiments (Randsborg 1995) (see Topic 4: Hjortspring Deposit). The double-prowed paddling boat of knot-free lime tree (suggesting organized forestry) develops from the vessels seen on cultic Bronze Age rock-carvings but is a deadly weapon in its own right, with a maximum speed of nearly 15 kilometres an hour, carrying 22 or more warriors up to 100-150 kilometres a day: necessarily an elite unit. Militia forces consisting of up to 25% of an entire Germanic population were mentioned by Caesar (Randsborg 1995: 185). Such forces were called upon to fight the large armies of Mediterranean societies. The military landscape included permanent lookout posts and underwater sea barriers: no part of the southern Baltic would have felt safe. Land barriers in the form of lines of pits with sticks at the bottom, in systems several hundred metres long, indicate battle fronts involving thousands of warriors and thus whole armies.

Interestingly, while other parts of Europe are full of large heavily fortified settlements and even towns during this period, Denmark has only a couple of lightly defended sites. The same is true in the following phases, which see only a few short wall systems, probably prepared battle-fields, to use military jargon. The lack of fortified towns in Denmark, akin to the *oppida* of France conquered by the Romans in Caesar's *Gallic War*, is a very interesting phenomenon. Clearly, territorial security must have relied on wide-ranging alliances coupled with mobile elite units – some of which were sea-faring – and stationary militia armies: the former primarily for attack, the latter primarily for defence. This type of organization both prevented and promoted the creation of larger social entities and eventually the Kingdom of Denmark.

As for the Mesolithic and Early Bronze Age, 'wet Denmark' has revealed crucial finds from this phase, in particular the bog-bodies: fully-preserved men, women and children who give us an idea of the physical appearance of the people of Denmark. Famous examples are Tollund Man (Fig. I.11) from around 400 BC, and Grauballe Man, probably from around 300 BC (Asingh and Lynnerup 2007). Full sets of clothing have also been preserved, like the fine woollen *peplos* worn by Huldremose Woman from the time of the birth of Christ. This woman also wore capes of fur and hide.

Relatively few conspicuous grave goods from the latter half of the first millennium BC have been found. However, the deposits include two four-wheeled wagons from Dejbjerg bog in West Jylland with elegant decorative bronze fittings, dated to very late in the millennium (Petersen 1888). The wagons and the style of their decorations have clear western European 'Celtic' parallels. Still more impressive is the famous Gundestrup silver cauldron, about 70 centimetres across and weighing 9 kilograms, from a bog in North Jylland, one the most prominent artefacts of pre-Roman Europe (e.g. Kaul 1995).

The Gundestrup cauldron consists of eight outer and five inner panels, a rounded bottom and a magnificent round bottom disc, all in relief. The outer panels depict torsos of male and female deities with animals and the like; the longer inner panels present a series of very interesting scenes including marching infantry and cavalry, horned deities, elephants, bulls, griffons, deer, a snake with ram's horns and so forth. The bottom disc depicts a huge wounded bull chasing dogs and an Amazon warrior. Some elements seem to be 'Celtic', that is Central and West European, while the animal kingdom, when real, presents eastern affinities. The overall style is 'Thracian', in other words Bulgarian (or Rumanian), but the group of artists working on the cauldron may have set up their workshop almost anywhere they could find a rich patron. Dating is another problem: the cauldron may have been made in the first century BC but it may also be older. The final puzzle is how it came to be in the North Jylland bog. Mercenaries may have been involved, perhaps Germanic tribes in Rumania, even the famous Cimbri who successfully fought the Romans until they met their defeat in the South of France in 101 BC. At any rate, in the 'Bauhaus' North, where decorations were almost non-existent on locally made items and structures, the Gundestrup cauldron must have been as shocking and fascinating as a horror film today.

Fig. I.13. Imperial Roman silver beakers, Hoby, Lolland. Early first century AD. After Friis-Johansen 1923.

In this competitive period, the Mediterranean societies of classical antiquity made their presence felt through alliances and trade. In contrast to the Bronze Age, contact often led to cultural opposition rather than imitation on the part of the peripheral partner. Germanic societies in Central Europe, for instance, only accepted Roman items that fitted into their own culture. Thus not a single perfume bottle crossed the Rhine. Even so, at the beginning of the first millennium AD a restricted elite group seems to have been seduced by the Roman life-style, as demonstrated by the splendid grave from Hoby on Lolland containing most of a Roman drinking set, including tableware in silver and bronze of Imperial quality: probably a political gift from a time when the Roman Empire had not completely abandoned the idea of further expansion towards the rivers Weser and Elbe, and even beyond (Friis-Johansen 1923) (Fig. I.13).

The motifs on the Hoby beakers refer to Homer's *Iliad*, including King Priam of Troy kneeling before the Greek hero Achilles to beg for the body of Hector, his slain son. On the beaker, Achilles is portrayed with the face of the Emperor Augustus, who is thus receiving a prominent 'Barbarian'. The motif echoes of Augustus' claim in his *Res gestae divi Augusti* ('The Achievements of the Divine Augustus') – which has survived on his temple in Ankara, Turkey (the *Monumentum Ancyranum*) – that the Germans begged the Emperor for peace. *Res gestae* states: 'My fleet sailed from the mouth of the Rhine eastwards as far as the lands of the Cimbri into which, up to that time, no Roman had ever penetrated either by land or by sea, and the Cimbri and Charydes and Semnones and other German peoples of that same region sought my friendship and that of the Roman people through their envoys.' How the beakers ended up on Lolland is an interesting question; they may have been acquired on that occasion or through other contacts, for instance emissaries to the Emperor or other dignitaries. Both of the Hoby beakers have the scribbled name of *Silius* (likely the original owner) on the bottom; between AD 14 and 21 a *C. Silius* was military commander (*legatus*) of the army of the upper Rhine with its headquarters at Mainz.

Later, princely burials rich in drinking glasses and other items manufactured in the western provinces of the Empire become widespread, but are found especially on the Danish islands, including Himlingeøje on eastern Sjælland (Lund Hansen 1995). Interestingly, stable isotope studies of male and female skeletons, from both rich and poorer graves (the true poor are largely unknown archaeologically), indicate that all ate the same beef-dominated diet with only insignificant amounts of fish and plant food. This is surprising given the existence of field systems (although the commonly grown barley may have been used for brewing beer). Nevertheless, from this period onwards loaves of bread were important grave gifts in Scandinavia.

Himlingeøje also has some of the earliest inscriptions in the Runic alphabet and may be its birthplace. Runes are a Germanic and probably a Danish invention, used where Latin letters would have functioned equally well. Germanic societies were clearly stressing their own identity *vis-à-vis* Rome.

Seemingly, a similar phenomenon was at work in the sphere of religion. Bronze Age people worshipped the sun and attempted to understand the apparent workings of the heavens. The sun may even have been perceived as a human being since a tall divine brimmed hat was placed on representations of the sun disc. The first clear indications of the existence of the Nordic pantheon, including Tyr and other deities known from the Icelandic Sagas, stem from pictures on gold bracteates of the fifth century AD. Tyr, or a similar German deity (*Mars Thingsus*), is named on Roman altars erected by Frisian auxiliaries in Roman service on Hadrian's Wall in England already by around AD 200. Likely, the Nordic pantheon was modelled on the Roman one, as indicated by translations, including the names of the days of the week.

A few recent finds suggest continuity between the Bronze Age (and beyond) and the late pagan period in terms of religion. On Bornholm some rock-caving panels from the Bronze Age have proved to have frames in front of them restricting access, almost like the altar area in churches. The panels also contain huge deposits from the Neolithic in hollows of the rock, suggesting that the rock itself was holy, not the rock-carvings. Furthermore, Late Iron Age structures have been found slap up against the same rocks; these, given their peculiar location, can hardly have had an economic function but are instead small special-purpose halls for particular rituals.

Phase V: Courts and Armies (250-700)

By now we have already passed the next caesura in Denmark's overall development, dating to the Late Imperial Period. During this critical phase, farmsteads grew substantially in size and large villages formed. A key archaeological site is Vorbasse in Jylland, but many other sites confirm this picture (Hvass 1986; cf. Hvass 1988) (Fig. I.14). At Vorbasse, extensive excavations have uncovered the development of a single settlement from shortly before the birth of Christ to the eleventh century, when the village moved to its present location some 100 metres away. One larger farmstead probably belongs to a local lord, possibly even the owner of the village, as indicated by a family cemetery with Roman imports. Interestingly, winter rye seems to have been introduced in the Late Imperial Period – securing the food supply – along with a number of other domesticated plants, including spices.

Centralized estates also developed. At Gudme – literally 'Gods' Home' – on eastern Fyn a compound was found with a large long-house, or hall, and a smaller special-purpose hall, together with a substantial number

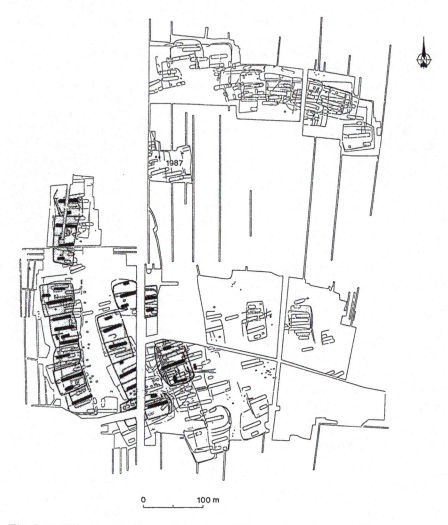

0   100 m

Fig. I.14. Village at Vorbasse, Jylland, *c*. 300 AD. After Hvass 1977.

of at least 60 wealthy farmsteads within a few square kilometres (the adjacent burial ground is the largest in Denmark) (Fig. I.15). Gudme is situated a few kilometres from a large coastal production site at Lundeborg and thus controlled traffic in the Store Bælt. Gudme – no doubt town-like in its heyday – was by far the largest settlement in Denmark; it has also yielded the largest concentration of small and large gold finds not only in Denmark but in all of northern Europe at this period. It is easy to imagine that large areas paid tribute to the king at Gudme.

Huge military bog-deposits with thousands of weapons, personal

Fig. I.15. Royal village of Gudme, Fyn, 300+ AD. Gudme is situated a few kilometres from a major contemporary emporium at Lundeborg on the coast of the Store Bælt. The manor house or palace (*storgård*) is surrounded by at least 60 farmsteads, possibly 100, but no doubt the whole district and more were tributary to the king. After Jensen 2001: vol. III.

equipment and even large rowing boats indicate regional struggles over the centuries, probably between kings. Most major deposits are found in the Lille Bælt region, possibly indicating East-West conflict, but the theatre of war may well have been larger with contenders coming from far afield. The military deposits provide a truly unique insight into the weaponry and fighting techniques of the age, as well as the garments and personal equipment of the soldiers; notably, trousers appear here for the first time.

Just one such find from Illerup bog in central Jylland (*c.* 200 AD) held more Roman sword-blades than have been found in the whole Roman Empire (Ilkjær 2000; cf. Jørgensen, Storgaard and Thomsen 2003). As at Hjortspring, the entire equipment of whole armies seems to have been deposited, allowing for a complete reconstruction of the warriors as they stood. Probably we are dealing in this case with amphibious swift elite troops, highly professional and with standardized equipment suggesting battle between pre-defined units. The forces may have numbered as much as 1,000 warriors, but evidently logistics would have set strict limits, at least for armies on the offensive.

At Illerup there are three levels of warriors: mounted high officers in fine garments and with ivory, gold and silver in their equipment, for instance on shield bosses; infantry officers with bronze shield-bosses and

31

swords; and common soldiers with iron shield-bosses and often only a lance and spear (and fighting knife). The ratio between the groups is about 1:8:64, each high commander having eight officers under him and each officer likely having eight privates under him, equivalent to a Roman tent group. Translated into ships, such a unit would have made up roughly the crew of two wide-keeled oak rowing boats of Nydam type, each carrying 36 rowers with other crew and passengers, and even horses. If the original force consisted of about 1,000 warriors, the actual number of boats was probably close to thirty, an impressive fleet indeed. Nydam is a weapons deposit from South Jylland; the boat in question has been dated to 310+ on the basis of dendrochronology. Incidentally, this find also comprises a pine boat, obviously originating north of Denmark.

From Ejsbøl in South Jylland comes a weapons deposit dating to about 300, also allowing us to determine the size of this unit. Nine mounted commanders have been identified, while there are 50 infantry swordsmen and 130 soldiers equipped with only a lance, together with a platoon of archers. Here the ratio differs from that at Illerup: 1:5:13, plus archers. This implies a different organizational structure with mounted warriors perhaps forming a tiny cavalry unit (for surprise attacks). If the warriors were not integrated into mixed weapons groups or even 'ships', the core of the army may have been a heavy company of swordsmen, supported by a couple of companies of lance fighters. The former would be decisive in attack but also formed a stable defensive unit. Such an organization would free six or more horsemen for the cavalry. Six boats of Nydam type could have carried the army to its region and field of battle.

Despite these weapons deposits, a clear indication of war, Denmark was an island of stability in a turbulent Europe during the fifth century. The country was even rich in gold, as demonstrated by the famous finely decorated Gold Horns from Gallehus in South Jylland dating to shortly after 400 (unfortunately stolen from the Royal Arts Chamber in 1802 and melted down). The Gold Horns weighed almost seven kilograms in all. Their decoration has never been interpreted; some motifs (such as dolphin riding) are clearly Roman while others have Nordic parallels; as to the content, domination is a theme, including the eating of another human being, but playful activities are also seen. Likely, the overall reference framework is religious (motifs clearly belong to Nordic mythology occur on contemporary gold bracteates). Perhaps some of the strangely folded figures are in fact hidden runes. At any rate, the horns carry the first longer Runic inscription, written in a traditional alliterated Nordic stanza: *Ek Hlewagastir, Holtijar, Horna, Tawido* ('I Lægæst, Holte's Son, the Horn, Made').

The gold reached Denmark as Roman payments for mercenaries and perhaps indirectly as Imperial payments for attacking 'kleptocrat' armies like that of the Huns. Gudme may have been the richest town in Denmark and northern Europe, but others flourished as well. The fact that grave-goods were scarce in this period is not an indication of poverty but rather of stable social conditions. With a single exception (see below), rich grave goods only reappear in the tenth century, the Late Viking Age – which saw the formation of a kingdom of 'all Denmark' – and a new dynasty with a need to assert itself. Characteristically, Viking graves very rarely contain items in silver or gold. These were family heirlooms, only found in hidden treasures.

This period was a complicated one for western Europe, seeing the centre of gravity of the Roman Empire move towards the east and Germanic 'empires' founded by warrior kings and their followers, like the Franks, conquer former Roman provinces and settle there. As far as Denmark is concerned, a new caesura does not occur until about 700.

Phase VI. Lords and Sea Kings (700-950)

Around 700 farmsteads again increased in size as demonstrated by Vorbasse village (Hvass 1986; cf. 1988). This change probably reflects a further rise in production spurred by a development in craft production and exchange. A series of mass production and market sites, often on the coasts, sprang up across north-western Europe (Ulriksen 1994) (Fig. I.16). Ribe in Denmark is one such site. Here the earliest mint in the country was established, with coins based on Frisian models. Perhaps Ribe is slightly misleading, since most of these production sites did not develop into medieval towns and cities. The manor house at Tissø on Sjælland helps to explain the rationale behind these production sites; they are as much a function of these complexes as stables, barns, and the fine hall and other important special-purpose structures, possibly for cult use. Incidentally, Tissø means 'Lake of Tyr', the aforementioned Nordic god of war. Craft production was obviously a way for estates to use their surplus in an international economy increasingly based on trade. The rise of Carolingian and Anglo-Saxon estates and trading settlements on the Rhine and around the English Channel should be seen in the same light.

The archaeological picture is anything but clear (due mainly to a lack of research), but it would seem that this development forms part of a much broader series of events, including the Muslim invasion of south-western Europe (links with the powerful Near Eastern economy), and the arrival of the Bulgars in south-eastern Europe (links with the trading empires of Central Asia). Even the slow rise of maritime towns in Italy at the same time may ultimately be linked to places such as Ribe and Tissø. The early Viking raids on western Europe, likely by Norwegians, may be seen as directed against these new centres of

Fig. I.16. Dates of emporia in north-western Europe. Note the contemporaneous emergence of many of them *c.* 700 AD. After Ulriksen 1994.

wealth, easily reached by the Nordic so-called 'Viking ship' with mast and sail, also originating in around 700 (cf. Fig. I.19).

The decades around 800 represent another peak period: Danish King Godfred was a contemporary of Charlemagne and King Offa of England (cf. Randsborg 1980). Muslim silver coins from Baghdad, Basra and other huge cities in the Abbasid Caliphate streamed into Scandinavia through Russia, only to disappear a few decades later. The Danes reacted to this decline by raiding western Europe. The armies of these sea-kings even settled in Danelagen (eastern England) and Normandy, leaving an imprint in the form of hundreds of place-names for their newly-won estates, like Rugby ('Rye village'), Derby ('Deer village') or Ivetôt ('Ivar's toft' or croft). The language of the Anglo-Saxons was heavily 'Danified'; 'love' comes from the Danish word meaning 'to promise'. Many French words are also Danish, like boulevard = bulwark ('*bulværk*'). The Normans even conquered England (in 1066); in the Mediterranean they won Sicily from the Muslims at about the same time.

Ultimately, Danelagen was recaptured by the English kings, perhaps indirectly helped by the fact that a new powerful influx of Muslim silver entered Scandinavia through Russia. These coins came from cities such as Samarkand and Buchara in Central Asia after the dramatic decline of Mesopotamia in the ninth century. Much Muslim silver must still have been in circulation when western Denmark took a new turn in the mid-tenth century.

At the emporium of Hedeby near the German border, an extremely rich chamber tomb was constructed in the mid-ninth century, seemingly for three men (Wamers 1994). A ship was placed above the wooden grave chamber, and above this a burial mound; slain horses were buried nearby. In the Early Viking Age it was not customary to use burial gifts, so this grave is truly special. The chamber contained three swords and other artefacts of costly Carolingian manufacture, probably princely ceremonial gifts. The grave may possibly be that of one of the Danish kings known to have had Frankish connections during this period, such as one of the mid-ninth-century kings named Horik, who permitted churches to be built at the emporia of Hedeby and Ribe. The stress on weapons, horses and expeditions (the ship) is an indication of high military status, perhaps death in battle.

In another royal ship-grave under a mound at Ladby on Fyn, the dead rested onboard the vessel; this grave also contained Carolingian items. The Ladby grave dates to *c.* 900 (Sørensen 2001). Later still are two princely burials at Søllested and Møllemosegård on Fyn, with wagons among numerous other expensive objects (Pedersen 1996). Søllested also contained a wax candle. These graves are contemporary with the chamber grave in the North Mound at Jelling in Jylland of the mid-tenth century.

If we examine the rune stones from the earlier Viking Age (before the mid-tenth century) we see a concentration in the central areas of Denmark, with others located close to the country's main roads, or even its highways. Rune stones are memorials erected over high-ranking individuals and probably indicate the transfer of position and property. Almost all are erected over men, probably at royal and elite manor houses. Their distribution may indicate that Fyn and Sjælland were the centres of gravity in the Early Viking Age, perhaps a distant reflection of the importance of the supreme Gudme centre in the Migration period and of other centres on the islands.

As noted above, early Denmark was a land almost completely devoid of fortified towns; territorial organization and alliances thus formed the basis for a kingdom which may have been born in blood, but was certainly vigilant. Large territories call for flexible and doubtless often competing leadership structures, with several 'kings', in other words the locally based military leaders of elite forces. Large territories also allow for joint action in force, for instance on plundering raids and even conquests abroad.

Phase VII. Kingdom Builders (950-1050)

An important royal palace was located at Jelling in Jylland in the tenth century: apparently in the middle of nowhere when seen through modern eyes, but right on the ancient northbound main road through the peninsula starting at Slesvig/Hedeby on the border (Randsborg 2008) (see Topic 5: Jelling Complex). Like a spider in the middle of its web, Jelling is also placed at the shortest possible distance from the largest number of main towns: Ribe, Århus, Viborg and Odense on Fyn, with Hedeby/Slesvig somewhat further away to the south.

Previously, this royal centre was known only from two colossal burial mounds; the northern mound probably had a Bronze Age mound as its core. A richly furnished wooden burial chamber was built inside the old mound in 959 (dendro-date). A southern companion mound was constructed in the 970s (dendro-dates). The southern mound is empty except for a huge stone V, probably part of a ship-setting. To the north of the northern mound another V has recently been found. If the two parts are joined together, the ship-setting must have been 354 metres long (exactly 1,200 Roman feet) and had the northern mound as its centre. The southern mound may be a symbolic 'protest', disturbing the ship-setting.

Exactly midway between the two mounds is a huge rune stone in its primary position (Fig. III.15). Next to it is a smaller rune stone, moved here from an unknown location. The latter was erected by 'King Gorm for his wife Thyra, the adornment of Denmark' (today's royal dynasty ultimately descends from King Gorm). The former was erected by 'King

Harald for his father Gorm and his mother Thyra; that Harald who won for himself all of Denmark and Norway and 'made the Danes Christian'. The stone has three main features: the main text; a fabulous monster fighting a snake above the line on Norway; and Christ on the cross above the line on Christianization.

Obviously this is an extremely important document. It should be considered alongside German written sources indicating that King Harald accepted Christianity between 962 and 965. The German Widukind, writing in 967-8, gives more details, including a demonstration of the powers of Christ through the carrying of red-hot iron and the statement that the Danes were Christians of old, but now accepted Christ as the only god. This is confirmed by a series of slightly later Danish coins with crosses. A rich grave at Mammen in North Jylland, dendro-dated to 970, contained a fine axe decorated with silver in the same animal style as King Harald's rune stone (Iversen 1991). This grave also held a wax candle and an extremely fine garment, partly made of silk, with gold and silver, perhaps a gift connected with a baptism (Ræder Knudsen 2007).

Unfortunately, the absolute chronology for the Danish kings during this crucial phase is uncertain. That King Harald succeeded Gorm is clear from the large Jelling rune stone of the 960s. If Gorm is connected with the northern mound and the ship-setting at Jelling, he died in around 958. If his wife Thyra (who died before Gorm) is linked with the mound, Gorm died a little later. Indeed, this truly unique monument must belong to a king. That Harald was followed by King Svend (died 1014) is also certain. Svend is mentioned from 994 (possibly 991) onwards, when he participated in new Norse attacks on England, ending with the Danish conquest. The son of Svend is King Knud (Canute) (died 1035) of England, Denmark and Norway.

Squeezed in between King Harald's rune stone and the northern mound is a Romanesque stone church from around 1100. Beneath it a series of large wooden churches have been found, the first – cathedral-sized – is archaeologically the oldest church in Denmark. Permission to build churches in the emporia of Hedeby and Ribe in South Jylland was granted by the Danish Kings Horik I and II (according to German written sources of the late ninth century), but these churches have not been found.

Under the wooden double basilica at Jelling is a chamber tomb containing the secondary burial of a man aged about 35-40 and some fine artefacts in the same style as those from the Mammen grave. It has been argued that this man is King Gorm, transferred here from the chamber in the northern mound which was opened in 964. However, it is more likely to be King Harald, who was deposed in a rebellion and died of his wounds in the lands of the Slavonians, where he was probably buried (cf. Lund 1998). This would fit in with the construction of the church by King Svend in the 980s, at the same time as the construction of the prestigious half-mile long two-lane bridge at Ravning Enge leading right up to Jelling. The building of bridges was considered a Christian act.

Recently, even the royal palace compound has been found, surrounded by a high, massive palisade fence north and south of the colossal ship-setting; the eastern and western parts of the fence have also been found, together with a number of halls. The palace at Jelling is several times larger than Denmark's previous largest manor house at Vorbasse. The palisade is so high that no one could see into the complex from the outside; notably, it was not built for defensive purposes.

The perfectly circular fortresses of Trelleborg type surrounding the core lands of western Denmark are truly impressive: Aggersborg (with a diameter of 240 metres) and Fyrkat (120 metres), built in around 980 (dendro-date) in northern Jylland; Nonnebakken (120 metres) at Odense on Fyn; and Trelleborg (136 metres, dendro-dated to the 970s and to 981), on western Sjælland (Olsen, Schmidt and Roesdahl 1977) (Fig. I.18). The inner part of the fortresses is occupied by large halls of identical size, four times four at Fyrkat and Trelleborg, twelve times four at Aggersborg. The status of the two or rather more circular fortresses in Skåne (such as at Trelleborg) is less clear since they do not present the same interior arrangement, but they are probably contemporary. No doubt royalty was behind these impressive projects, likely King Svend, who 'fenced his camp' according to an early eleventh-

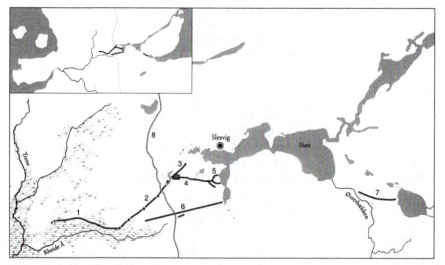

Fig. I.17. Danevirke defence wall system (sea barriers excluded). After H.H. Andersen 1998. 1 = curved wall; 2 = main wall; 3 = north wall; 4 = connection wall; 5 = walls at Hedeby; 6 = Kovirke; 7 = east wall, 8 = main north-south road through Jylland. (Dots in 2 = Danish redoubts from 1864.)

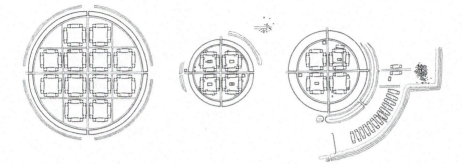

Fig. I.18. Trelleborg-type fortresses: (*left to right*) Aggersborg, Fyrkat, Trelleborg. After Olsen et al. 1977.

century poetic source (*Encomium Emmae Reginae*) composed for Queen Emma, his Norman daughter-in-law.

In the south of Jylland a series of long fortification walls known as Danevirke, designed to protect Denmark's short continental border from southern attack, dates to the late seventh century; one specific phase is dated to 737 (dendro-date), another (reinforced with boulders) is somewhat later (a written source credits King Godfred with the construction of Danevirke in 808) (H.H. Andersen 1998) (Fig. I.17). Interestingly, the Kanhave channel across the island of Samsø in the Kattegat, providing ships with a western exit from the natural harbour of Stavnsfjord (opening towards the east), is dated to 726 (dendro-date). The channel should be regarded as part of a defensive system protecting Denmark from northern attack.

A wall connecting Danevirke with the fortifications around the emporium of Hedeby to the east of Danevirke is dendro-dated to the 960s, the reign of King Harald. The dead-straight single-phase wall south of Hedeby (known as Kovirke), joining with Danevirke to the west, belongs to the same period as the circular Trelleborg fortresses judging from some construction details. The Kovirke system was never repaired or improved and is thus a single-event structure. The wall has been Carbon-14 dated to the (late) tenth century.

A contemporary German written source relates that German King Heinrich I defeated Danish King Gnupa in 934; Gnupa is also mentioned on rune stones from Hedeby (as the father of a King Sigtryg). Bishops of Slesvig, Ribe and Århus were appointed as early as 948, but do not seem to have entered Denmark; the appointments were intended to bolster the weak archbishopric of Hamburg. Bishops of the same cities and of Odense were appointed by Emperor Otto III in 988, when the Danish king had already accepted Christianity. In fact, the size of the first church at Jelling may indicate a Danish plan of the 980s for a bishop of Jylland with his seat at Jelling.

We know of an attack on Denmark by Emperor Otto II in 974 from a very slightly later German written source, Thietmar (975-1018). It is said that the Danes were 'manning the ditch made for the defence of the country and the gateway called Wieglesdor', and that the Germans were conquering 'all fortifications'. 'Wieglesdor' is probably German for Vigleksdør ('-*dør*' meaning gateway, cf. door). Viglek is a Danish Saga king whose Latin name is Wiglecus (Saxo IV.2.1). According to Saxo, Wiglecus was angry that Amled (Latin Amlethus, cf. Shakespeare's Hamlet) had conquered Jylland. So Wiglecus killed Amlethus in battle with support from Sjælland and Skåne. Viglek's son was Vermund, whose son Uffe in turn fought the Germans on the River Ejder, the border south of Danevirke (Saxo IV.4). A gateway in Danevirke, or more accurately in Kovirke, was evidently named with reference to these tales as well as to contemporary events.

Thietmar also reports that 'in these regions [the emperor] constructed a stronghold with a permanent garrison'. Such a stronghold is unknown archaeologically and may have been built south of the River Ejder. There is no evidence that any part of Jylland was occupied by the Germans. Two rune stones for fallen officers of King Svend's personal guard erected on open ground between Hedeby and Kovirke may even stand on the battlefield. For 983 Thietmar reports that a stronghold, 'strengthened by Emperor Otto II against the Danes', was conquered by the latter upon the death of Otto II. 983 was also the year of the great Slavonian revolt that drove the Germans back across the Elbe until the early twelfth century and gave the Danes ample peace to conquer England.

The rune stones of the mid-tenth century are clustered in the Jelling region of Central Jylland and North Jylland with a small 'outpost' on the island of Lolland (Randsborg 1980). In around 1000 rune stones are still concentrated in North Jylland, with the addition of Skåne; none are found in Central Jylland. There are a few rune stones at Hedeby/Slesvig, all 'historical' (mentioned above). King Knud, son of Svend, may be mentioned on a late rune stone from Skåne. After the reign of Knud, rune stones are found almost exclusively on the island of Bornholm; in style they resemble the Swedish rune stones of the eleventh century. Bornholm is often a deviant area in archaeological terms. A written source from the close of the ninth century (Ottar) claims that Bornholm has its own king, while the same source seems to indicate that peripheral Halland (the province on the Kattegat Sea to the north of Skåne) belonged to Denmark.

Most inscriptions on early rune stones are short and often difficult to read. The later stones of the later tenth century all subscribe to the formula 'X erected this stone over Y' with various additions, in particular family relations, but also titles and occupations, adjectives like *god*/'good' (well-born) and so on, Pagan and Christian religious symbols or conjurations, and a fair number of other elements such as place names. The late rune stones from around 1000 specify many non-family relations, like *fælle/*'fellow' (someone with whom one shares property). The late stones are easier to read, in particular since words are separated. In terms of structure there is a striking resemblance between the texts on rune stones and the written deeds known from the contemporary Anglo-Saxon world drawn up in connection with transfers of position, land and other property.

Rune stones were probably erected to sanction specific contracts, for instance a family taking over land traditionally belonging to another lineage or, as at Jelling, members of the royal family establishing themselves in Central Jylland to become kings of 'all Denmark', effectively of an empire. The changing distributions of the rune stones over time confirms the theory of a changing social geography. Once a new position or ownership is acknowledged, there is no need for further memorials, since reference to the rune stone would suffice.

Finally, Jelling did not develop into a major town in line with the cities of the eleventh century; indeed, the distribution of towns in 1100 is almost identical to that of the present. Jelling may have been a sort of 'capital' for a generation or so in the tenth century, but that was all. In around 1000 the focus was on Sjælland and Skåne, with the new city of Lund – Denmark's London and future seat of Scandinavia's first archbishop.

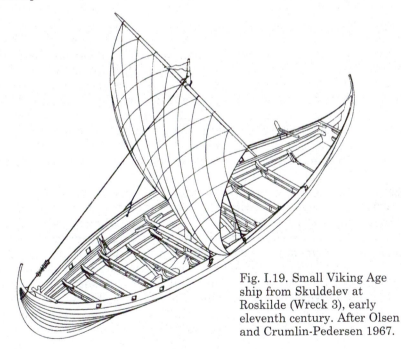

Fig. I.19. Small Viking Age ship from Skuldelev at Roskilde (Wreck 3), early eleventh century. After Olsen and Crumlin-Pedersen 1967.

Denmark held sway over England until 1042. In 1027 King Knud visited Rome together with the German Emperor; he and his son King Hardeknud are buried at Winchester. Hardeknud, who died without heirs, was the last of the Danish kings of England. After the death of Knud in 1035, Norway elected Magnus king; upon the death of Hardeknud, Magnus also won the Danish throne (reign: 1042-47). Magnus' rival King Svend Estridsøn (reign: 1047-74) was the son of one of King Knud's sisters; he appears to have been a modernizer, not least in terms of the church. Five of Svend's sons became kings of Denmark; the fourth, Erik Ejegod (reign: 1095-1103), died on Cyprus on pilgrimage to the Holy Land. Erik became the progenitor of the 'Valdemars', the great Danish kings of the late twelfth century onwards who held sway over northern Germany and conquered the northern part of Estland (Estonia) during the Second Danish Crusade at the beginning of the thirteenth century.

Phase VIII. Christian Modernizers (1050-1200)

A map of Denmark's cities in 1100 is also a map of some of the most important investments made by the elites: wooden and stone cathedrals and other churches on the crofts of town manor houses belonging to aristocrats, bishops and kings, the adjacent craft workshops, markets, mints and so on (see Map 2). An idea of the economic power behind the provincial capitals and other emerging towns is provided by the huge manor house of the last phase of Vorbasse in the eleventh century (albeit smaller than the tenth-century royal palace at Jelling) (Fig. I.20). At Lisbjerg near Århus the hall on a similar large croft (with palisade) was replaced by a wooden church and shortly afterwards by the current stone church of the early twelfth century. Thus a priest must have been present on the estate. At the Østergård manor house in South Jylland, with a two-storey palatial bay-hall dating from around 1100, jewellery, probably of imperial German manufacture, has been found.

The cities of the eleventh century – Slesvig, Ribe, Århus, Viborg, Odense, Roskilde and Lund – are still among Denmark's most populous, although several trading towns which sprang up in the Late Middle Ages, including Flensborg, København and Malmø, have become very important. They all testify to a strong continuity of settlement throughout the past millennium. Ordinary villages, which moved slightly within their defined territories right up to the eleventh century, have also remained in the same place since the close of the Viking Age, a fact which creates problems for archaeological recording and excavation. Only the most recent developments in settlement patterns (after World War II) have modified this picture. In the late medieval period København became the capital, situated near the population median in the increasingly important Øresund region. Øresund is the

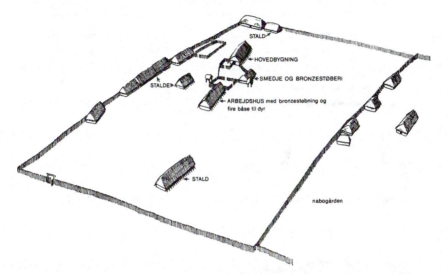

Fig. I.20. Main farmstead at Vorbasse village, Jylland. Early eleventh century.
After Birkebæk 1982. *Nabogården* = neighbouring farmstead; *Stald(e)* = sta-
ble(s); *Arbejdshus med bronzestøbning og fire båse til dyr* = work building with
bronze-casting and four stalls for animals; *Smedje og bronzestøberi* = smithy
and bronze foundry; *Hovedbygning* = main building (hall).

main thoroughfare between the North Sea, the Kattegat and the Baltic
(see Map 1).

A chart of excavated Danish house structures from between 1000 and
1200 shows a decline in the number of buildings (the result of villages
moving to their present location) up to about 1100 (see Table 3 on p.
149). This is also when the traditional three-aisled farm longhouses
and the fairly common adjacent pit-houses used for craft-working
disappeared. The magnificent so-called Trelleborg halls with oblique
outer support braces, which appeared only in the late tenth century,
also vanished. However, their spacious interior rooms without roof
support posts were fashionable in the early medieval period, as shown
in the same chart by the one-aisled houses and buildings on
rectangular stone foundations, particularly common after 1100. Two-
aisled structures, emerging in the tenth century, and fine projection-
or bay-houses are also common after 1100.

As indicated by manor houses like Lisbjerg, the wooden churches of
the early Christian period functioned as private chapels for the elites. In
several cases, manor houses have been uncovered next to the stone
churches built above wooden ones. At Hørning near Århus a small
wooden church, probably from the third quarter of the eleventh century
(a decorated wooden board has survived), was found under the
Romanesque stone church. Beneath the wooden church was a chamber
tomb for a prominent Late Viking Age woman, originally under a

43

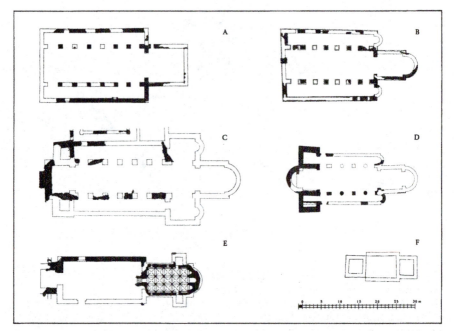

Fig. I.21. Early stone churches of the eleventh century in Denmark. (A) Holy Cross, Dalby, Skåne; (B) Our Lady, Roskilde, Sjælland; (C) Roskilde Cathedral, Sjælland; (D) Asmild near Viborg, North Jylland; (E) St Nicolai, Århus (cathedral), Jylland; (F) St Jørgensbjerg Church, Roskilde, Sjælland: one of the earliest archaeologically known stone churches in Denmark, *c.* 1040. After Johannsen and Smidt 1981.

mound. After the mound had been levelled, the church was constructed in such a way that the short western side of the chamber was flush with the western end of the church. Obviously it was important for Christian descendants to demonstrate a connection with their probably heathen ancestor of three generations earlier.

Wooden churches may well have been used throughout this phase. The first stone churches were built in the early eleventh century (Fig. I.21). Excavations in St Jørgensbjerg Church near Roskilde have uncovered the foundation trenches of a small stone church in travertine; this was demolished and its stone blocks reused to build the present church, probably in the late eleventh century (Olsen 1960). The foundations of the first stone church can be dated by a hoard of 104 coins, the latest 61 from the early years of King Hardeknud's reign (1035-42). Excavations next to the church uncovered the manor house. Another very early stone church has been found in Lund (Cinthio 2004).

Travertine was commonly used to build the very early stone churches from before and around 1100 (Randsborg 2003). Dendro-chronology is of enormous help in dating these but mostly we are left with the stylistic

Fig. I.22. Fresco (detail) from Ørreslev (Ørridslev) Church, Jylland, *c.* 1100. Photo: Author.

dates of frescos and various architectural elements, alongside occasional historical information. The only stone church with a dated inscription is granite Gjellerup in West Jylland, of 1140. A detailed survey of the evidence is informative.

The earliest surviving frescos are Byzantine in style and belong to a travertine church at Gundsømagle near Roskilde; they have parallels in

Greece in around 1050 and in Austria in the 1080s (Græbe et al. 1990). The choir of Gundsømagle Church is dendro-dated to (shortly) 'after 1083'. The frescos in Væ Church in Skåne have Italian parallels in around 1100, French parallels from the beginning of the twelfth century, German parallels in the 1120s, and English parallels around 1130. Væ is historically dated to before 1121. The second phase of the magnificent granite and travertine twin-spired Tveje Merløse Church on Sjælland – with frescos from around 1150 – is dendro-dated to 'after 1133'. Asperup Church on Fyn (no frescos) is dendro-dated to 1170. Tamdrup Church in Jylland is dendro-dated to 'after 1084'; the frescos are contemporary with those in the stone church at Jelling and have continental European parallels in the second half of the eleventh century. Ørreslev Church in Jylland, with similar frescos, is dendro-dated to '(after) 1100' (Fig. I.22). A dendro-date from the beautiful early travertine monastery church at Veng in East Jylland gave 'after 1045', likely the last third or quarter of the eleventh century (de Fine Licht and Michelsen 1988-89: 3195, 3213, 3250 n. 36). Dendro-dates for the roof-timbers of stone churches near Ribe in South Jylland have yielded surprisingly late dates, the earliest 'after 1155', seemingly in accordance with Gjellerup Church above (Madsen 2003).

Written sources mention that Estrid, King Knud's sister, built a 'stone church', perhaps the first in Denmark, in Roskilde in 1026/7 to commemorate her slain husband Ulf, killed by King Knud. (The aforementioned St Jørgensbjerg is probably an off-shoot of this project.) Beneath today's Roskilde Cathedral is a single large travertine church commonly ascribed to Bishop Nordmand (acting 1073-88), who died on Rhodes during a pilgrimage to the Holy Land. From a written source it is known that the frescos in this church were repainted under Nordmand's successor Bishop Arnold (acting 1088-1124). However, the lower parts of the long walls of this church belong to an earlier structure, probably Estrid's church (Olsen 1960: 29).

Several large stone churches date to the mid- or late eleventh century, including Dalby and Lund in Skåne, Roskilde (several), Ringsted, Slagelse on Sjælland, Odense on Fyn, and Århus (St Nicolai, now Our Lady). There is a notable concentration in the eastern regions of Denmark. The standing Romanesque cathedrals of Lund, Roskilde, Viborg and Ribe (only fragments of the early church in Slesvig survive) belong to the early (to mid-) twelfth century.

The first monasteries in Denmark belonged to the Benedictine order and were founded in the late eleventh century; the Cistercians followed in the twelfth century. The mendicant orders of the Franciscans (very important) and Dominicans, concentrating in towns, followed in the early thirteenth century. Among the less important orders in Denmark are the Carmelites; they, like the Brigittines (a Nordic order), reached Denmark only in the fifteenth century.

The Knights Hospitallers or Knights of St John were called upon and supported by King Valdemar I (reign: 1154-82). The battle dress and flag of the fighting wing of this order are red with a white cross, identical to the Danish royal and national ensign since the Middle Ages. One of the largest and most impressive castles of the Middle Ages, Crac des Chevaliers in Syria, was built by the Knights of St John (1150+). A Danish parallel is huge Hammershus on Bornholm of the close of the twelfth century, no doubt built with the Danish crusades in the Baltic in mind, although there is no known connection with the Knights of St John; in fact, we have no early sources at all on Hammershus, an all too common problem in Denmark (Fig. I.24).

Denmark's Romanesque church frescos are magnificent; international in style, they form an extremely important part of the country's medieval heritage. Equally interesting are the hundreds of fine Romanesque stone reliefs such as portals, an integral part of church architecture but strangely overlooked internationally (Mackeprang 1948). Stone baptismal fonts, decorated in the same evocative style as the reliefs, are very common – almost 2,000 are known in separate regional groups; these also deserve new attention (Mackeprang 1941). Wooden crucifixes and altars have also survived from the first Christian centuries, including a unique series of so-called golden altars from the twelfth century with complex painted decorations (Nørlund 1928). Unfortunately, only a very few complete stained glass windows have survived (though we have large numbers of shards): a glimpse of how the light of Paradise must have been perceived in the Early Middle Ages.

The art of brick-making and building arrived in the mid-twelfth century (probably directly from northern Italy) and was first used in the church of Ringsted on Sjælland – the burial place of the royal Valdemar lineage – and then in the church of the Cistercian monastery at Sorø on Sjælland, built by Absalon (born 1128) bishop of Roskilde (1158-1201) and archbishop of Lund (1178-1201). In Skåne, Absalon inaugurated the beautiful all-brick church at Gumløse in 1191, accompanied by the archbishop of Nidaros (Trondheim) in Norway and the bishop of Växjö in Sweden (Fig. I.23). Construction of Roskilde's magnificent brick cathedral was similarly initiated by Absalon, probably also responsible for the introduction of Gothic architectural features to Denmark. At Bjernede on Sjælland, a round church was begun in stone but completed in brick; obviously this new material was perceived as very attractive from the mid-twelfth century onwards.

Absalon – a medieval Danish Richelieu – continued to hold his Roskilde see even when he became archbishop of Lund. He died in 1201 after an eventful life, including several years of study in Paris as a young man. From King Valdemar I, his foster brother, he acquired 'Havn' (harbour), later København, where he built a fortress in the 1160s (the ruins can still be seen beneath Christiansborg Castle, now

Fig. I.23. Gumløse Church, Skåne, built of brick and inaugurated in the early
1190s. Drawing and plan. After Kornerup 1866.

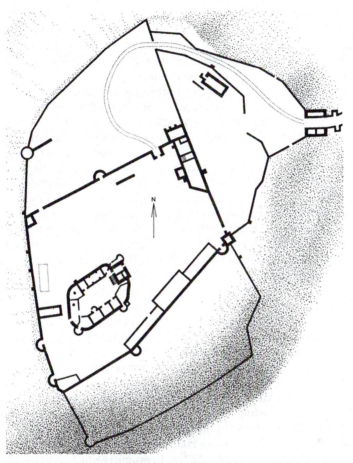

Fig. I.24. Hammershus Castle, Bornholm, close of the twelfth century: a Danish 'Crac des Chevaliers' overlooking the Baltic. North to south: 330 metres. After R.A. Olsen 1996.

the Danish Parliament). Absalon was also instrumental in the First Danish Crusade and the final conquest in 1168 of the island of Rygen in North Germany, inhabited by pagan Slavonians (an attempted conquest in 1136 failed). Less happy were Absalon's relations with the inhabitants of Skåne, who rebelled in protest against new taxes.

Absalon also charged his scribe Saxo 'Grammaticus' (*c.* 1160-1208+), educated in France, with the composition of a *Gesta Danorum*, a modern history of the Danes aimed at strengthening the country's European reputation: a magnificently detailed work and a major source for the twelfth century in particular. There is nothing comparable to this work during this period anywhere in northern Europe.

The eleventh to twelfth centuries produced no parallels to the magnificent circular Trelleborg fortresses of the late tenth century. Strongholds are now far less regular in shape and less conspicuous, but still built of earth and wood. All belong to the king or to the very highest echelons of society. The earliest stone fortification is the truly impressive round travertine tower at Bastrup on Sjælland from around 1100, the largest tower in Europe at this period (Randsborg 2003). The earliest military structure in brick is the final phase – the front brick wall – of Danevirke built by King Valdemar I (reign: 1154/7-1182). Brick fortification towers also begin to appear in the late twelfth century. Other military structures include Absalon's castle at Havn with its limestone curtain wall and Vordingborg Castle guarding the main naval harbour on the westernmost Baltic. Kalundborg on western Sjælland has been called a Danish Carcassonne; the superb and highly original church – a symbol of the Heavenly Jerusalem – has five octagonal spires. Dating to the very late twelfth century is the large and magnificent Hammershus on a high coastal rock on Bornholm: as mentioned, it was a base for Danish activities in the eastern Baltic, including conquests in pagan Estland (Estonia) shortly after 1200 (Fig. I.24). Fortresses include inland Søborg (with an adjacent township) and Gurre, both in North Sjælland, and Lilleborg on Bornholm.

In the light of late prehistoric armies including 1,000 or more elite warriors, extremely large militia forces engaging in battle across kilometre-long fronts and Viking Age armies conquering lands such as England, we might expect the early medieval armies to be even larger. Certainly militia forces could still be substantial, but due to physical and logistical constraints they operated for only limited periods at a time. Mostly they were not operational and military duties were gradually replaced by taxes in a relatively secure Denmark. A new development was the increasing role played by the cavalry, difficult and costly to maintain, and obviously the prerogative of the nobility. At the great civil war battle of Fodevig in Skåne in 1134, some 300 German mercenary knights were decisive in a battle between large militia forces. 'Five bishops and sixty priests' fell in the battle, according to Saxo. This is reminiscent of the Battle of Hastings in 1066, where William of Normandy's knights won the field from the tired infantry of the English King Harold, as shown on the Bayeux Tapestry. The 'armies' of this phase could be as small as a platoon of mounted warriors, armed family members and house carls, alongside allies with forces of identical composition, possibly with additional peasant or other dependent infantry: inviting and engaging in feuding rather than battle (Lund 1996).

Inscriptions on a lead tablet from the grave of King Valdemar I in Ringsted Church represent an interesting piece of psychological history of this phase (cf. Carelli 2001: 440f.). The tablet contains two versions of what is essentially the same inscription: one factual, the other a slightly later version modified with quotes from Svend Aggesøn's forerunner of Saxo's famous *Gesta Danorum*, the *Brevis Historia Regum Daciae* of the close of the twelfth century. The back, presenting the original text, reads: 'Here rests the king of the Danes Valdemar I, conqueror and ruler of the Slavonians, liberator of the fatherland, protector of the peace, who, son of Holy [King] Knud, conquered the inhabitants of Rygen and first converted them to belief in Christ. But he died in the 1182nd year after the incarnation of the Lord, in the 26th year of his reign, 4th (day before) *Idus Maji* [i.e. 12 May].' The front, with the slightly later version from the end of the twelfth century, reads: 'Here rests the king of the Danes Valdemar I, son of Holy [King] Knud, mighty conqueror of the Slavonians, eminent liberator of the suppressed fatherland, restorer and preserver of the peace. He happily defeated the inhabitants of Rygen and first converted them to belief in Christ, destroying their idols. He also first erected the wall protecting the entire kingdom, generally called Danevirke, made of burned brick and built the stronghold on Sprogø. But he died in the 1182nd year after the incarnation of the Lord, in the 26th year of his reign, 4th [day before] *Idus Maji* [i.e. 12 May].'

In the second version, King Valdemar appears in an almost Baroque and clearly Christian light as the good shepherd of his people while simultaneously dealing forcefully with Denmark's enemies: the ideal image of a medieval monarch at the time of the Second Crusade. Certainly, compared to the inscription on King Harald's rune stone at Jelling, the family element is toned down with respect to the Christian element; there is also a new sentimental tone. In fact, the accomplishments of King Valdemar were limited compared to those of King Harald and the other early members of the dynasty which led Denmark from prehistory to medieval Europe, created an empire and protected the kingdom.

Contemporary law codes are of great interest for their information on both social conditions and ways of thinking. Valdemar I's grandson, Valdemar II (reign: 1202-41), promulgated a new Law of Jylland in 1241 opening with the powerful stanzas: 'With law shall the land be built. But if everyone were satisfied with his own and let others enjoy the same rights, no law would be needed.' One particular clause (II.112) states: 'If a man finds silver or gold, either in mounds or after his plough, or in any other way, then the king shall have it. But if he denies that he found it, he must defend himself with an oath among his friends.'

This clause reveals that valuable archaeological finds were frequently discovered and that they were the property of the king, in other words of the kingdom; this forms the basis for all subsequent antiquarian regulation in Denmark. As Saxo tells us, the Danish kings also took a more intellectual interest in the past; King Valdemar I even sent out an expedition to study cracks in a rock considered by some to be a runic inscription. Saxo himself includes many archaeological notes, including those on megalithic tombs and ancient field systems ('in forests') 'demonstrating that Denmark used to have a much larger population'; he also reports on the excavation of Bronze Age mounds.

In the Late Middle Ages, the Danish kings took an interest in preserving and restoring churches. In the early seventeenth century all prehistoric and other monuments in both Denmark and Norway were recorded parish by parish on the king's orders (Randsborg 1994). Instrumental in this process was Ole Worm, who also created – and published – his own museum, as well as the runic inscriptions from the Viking Age and one of the Gold Horns from the Migration Period. Unfortunately, he failed to publish the other information he had collected, most of which was lost in the great København fire of 1728. Thus an era of archaeological and historical investigation also began in our Phase VIII.

Conclusions

In what follows, our Anatomy of Denmark will continue through the centuries up to the present, but we will first pause to cast a brief glance at the highlights of earlier periods, extensively supported by archaeology. Below, the voices of historians of the written word – be it on parchment, paper, newspaper or in the electronic media – will play a greater role. However, a material dimension and approach are maintained, stressing physical and thus visual culture. The plan to devote more or less equal attention to all phases will also be adhered to in the interest and respect of all forms of cultural expression.

Denmark has a very long and illustrious archaeological research tradition which at first concentrated on burials and deposits of often very conspicuous artefacts. Today, Danish archaeology has yielded unique information on the development and nature of settlements, including the halls of the Bronze Age and the final phase of prehistory. The Danish bogs and other wet environments, including the cores of Bronze Age mounds, have been benign to the preservation of organic materials, including human bodies, clothing, wagons and boats.

Denmark has a large quantity of informative data on the very long hunter-gatherer phase (before 4000 BC). It has a truly impressive collection of megalithic monuments – dolmens and passage graves – of the early food-producing phase before 3000 BC. And it has a splendid, in some respects even unique, Bronze Age (in particular the fourteenth century BC). The Iron Age – from 500 BC onwards – is composite but also rich in finds, often of European origin, including Roman artefacts. The deposits comprise fine weapons and even the equipment of whole armies and their vessels.

The Late Iron and Viking Ages are complex and have similarly provided a wealth of data on aspects such as the rise of mass production and trade, Denmark's naval history, the formation of the Kingdom of Denmark and the introduction of Christianity. The Early Middle Ages ('High Middle Ages' in European terminology) is another peak period for Denmark, seeing the erection of many wooden churches, thousands of Romanesque parish churches in stone, and fine cathedrals. Today's system of villages became established during this period (the late eleventh century), which also saw the foundation of towns and cities –

as towns and cities. Denmark was finding its place among the European nations and powers, bending to circumstances rather than creating them. The Viking Age may seem an aberration, but is indicative of foreign engagement and interest, even concern for other people, as a characteristically Danish quality.

Part II

History: 1200 AD to Today

I Danmark er jeg født, dér har jeg hjemme,
der har jeg rod, derfra min verden går.

In Denmark I was born, there is my home,
there lie my roots, from there my world takes off.
Hans Christian Andersen, 1850

Introduction

Written sources become more plentiful towards the close of the twelfth century, and this may encourage the feeling that later periods can be studied without taking into consideration the material world, as in so many works on Denmark's history. This is certainly not the case. However, it would be equally unwise to ignore written data in this second part. The ambition is to place as much weight as possible on the man-made material world – as described above – in presenting Danish history over the last 800 years. The main purpose of this is to integrate this portrait with that of earlier historical phases, but it is also important to emphasize an aspect overlooked or even ignored by the academic world. The non-written evidence of human activity and intelligence is not a standard subject taught at school or university: both institutions which have evolved from the literary tradition of the medieval church.

Defining Denmark
(see also above, p. 3)

The 'Denmark' considered hitherto is the southernmost part of Scandinavia or 'Old Denmark'. The loss of the eastern provinces and in particular Skåne in 1658 (the island of Bornholm was regained) was a terrible shock to the kingdom. However, to be politically correct, ignore the 'east' and concentrate on Denmark within its present borders would be a grave cultural mistake. Nevertheless, the eastern parts of Denmark, now provinces of Sweden, naturally play a smaller role in the sections on recent times, as Swedish state interests have become paramount (cf. Johannesson 1981). Interestingly, however, with the new Øresund Bridge between København and Malmø (and with Europe at peace), these once separate entities are again becoming naturally integrated, perhaps as freely as in the distant past: a not uncommon process throughout the European Union but unfortunately all too rare elsewhere.

A similar, though smaller, problem exists at the foot of Jylland where Denmark shares a border with Germany, to which it lost Slesvig (and Holstein) in 1864, before regaining a substantial part of the province after World War I. In the Late Middle Ages, Slesvig was administratively integrated with German Holstein, despite Danish domination; this created endless problems. Interestingly, after World War II northern Germany has looked to Denmark for cultural inspiration. Today the North German police take Danish lessons and many Germans, like East Europeans (and Swedes), work in Denmark, which has one of the strongest economies in the world. Today, Swedes attempt to speak Danish, something which never happened 20 years ago.

The former Danish possessions in the Baltic are not covered in this work. These include (apart from occasional mainland German principalities): the island of Rygen from the twelfth to the thirteenth century (onwards), Gotland (fourteenth to seventeenth centuries), Øsel (sixteenth to seventeenth centuries) and parts of mainland Estland (Estonia) from the early thirteenth to the fourteenth century.

Norway – united with Denmark in a new imperial entity from the late fourteenth century until the Vienna Congress in 1815, when it was ceded to Sweden (a declaration of independence was annulled) – is a separate country not dealt with here. Norway regained its independence in 1905. In fact, the so-called Nordic Kalmar Union under Danish leadership existed, with some interruptions, from the close of the fourteenth century (1397) until the early sixteenth century. Also omitted from this account are Danish overseas possessions in India, West Africa and the Caribbean (the Virgin Islands were ceded to the USA in 1917). The same is true of the North Atlantic nations: Greenland, Iceland, the Faroe Islands and so on, gained by Denmark alongside Norway in the fourteenth century, but which remained Danish after 1815 (Iceland became independent during World War II).

Population

An important but difficult issue to tackle is the size of Denmark's population and its distribution: the number of farmers and craftworkers, sailors, soldiers and so forth. The size of the population is a relative measure of productivity, taxable property and income, and so on. In the Middle Ages there were a total of 2,700 parish churches in the countryside, towns and cities (Wienberg 1993) (see Map 2 on p. x and Table 4 on p. 150). The vast majority of these churches were built during the Romanesque period. Maps show that churches concentrate in more fertile areas, supporting larger populations and as such can be used as indicators of population numbers and densities. Similarly, the number of churches in cities and towns are indicators of their size and importance (Andrén 1985).

With an average population in each parish of 300-400 people, the total (adult) population of the country would have been close to one million in the twelfth century (cf. Christensen 1938). The province of Halland is the only area for which we have reliable data. Halland had 9,206/9,336 'farmers' (*rustici*) in 660 settlements with (roughly) 92 churches in the early thirteenth century. This gives about 100 farmers per church/parish (and about 14 per settlement); to this number we should add their family and other individuals (possibly 2-3 adults per 'farmer'), alongside various other groups.

In the late eleventh century, Adam of Bremen gives the number of churches in the various regions as 300 in Skåne, 150 on Sjælland, 100 on Fyn and, probably, 150 in Jylland (Adam: 14, 204, 244). The rather high number for Skåne may include churches in Halland and Blekinge. Information provided by the Icelandic *Knytlinge Saga* of the early thirteenth century on the number of churches and 'ships' in the dioceses of Denmark confirms this picture (Bekker-Nielsen 1977: Book 32). The *Knytlinge Saga* claims to describe conditions during the reign of King Knud (1014/18-35), but its information in fact concerns the twelfth century. A strong correlation between the number of churches and 'ships' can be seen. A 'ship' in this context is not a vessel but a unit of land of sufficient size to build, equip and man a warship.

For earlier periods only archaeology can provide an estimate. In the Mesolithic, the population density was no doubt very low, on average a few people per square kilometre. The high number of megalithic tombs of the late fourth millennium (40,000 in present-day Denmark alone) must reflect a population running into several hundreds of thousands. The mounds of the Early Bronze Age give the same impression. An Iron Age population of a half to one million people does not seem unrealistic on the basis of settlements. Fluctuations are likely, for instance in connection with the Black Death of the 1340s and later, but these are blurred by fluctuations in settlement patterns and the growth of the towns in the Late Middle Ages, among other factors. As to the impact of the Black Death, estimates vary enormously for rural settlements, but no towns were founded in Denmark during the half century following the plague. 83 towns were founded before 1350 (three-quarters of these between 1200 and 1350) and more than one third of that in the period 1400-1550 (see Table 6 on p. 152).

Only in a very few early cases do we have crucial sequential information. One example is the village of Hørve on Sjælland, which in the Middle Ages belonged to the Bishop of Roskilde (see Table 5 on p. 151). The amount of rent paid and the nature of the farms are known. In 1290, the village had 12 farms and paid 220 barrels of grain. In 1370 the village also had 12 farms and paid 210 barrels (no reduction due to the Black Death). In 1591, after the Protestant Reformation, the village had 21 farms but paid only 126 barrels of grain to the owner. It is likely that the rearing of cattle and horses had become more important and that this is the uncertain factor. Another issue is the amount of work delivered at the large farms and even nearby Dragsholm Castle, in particular by small farmers. These findings are confirmed by the village of Farum on Sjælland, also owned by the Bishop of Roskilde, as concerns the supposed decrease in size of large farms and the tendency to create equal-sized farmsteads in the village over time.

It has been estimated that the population of Denmark reached 825,000 (600,000 not counting the eastern Skåne provinces) in 1645, likely a substantial decline from the High Middle Ages (Ladewig Petersen 1980: 41f.). 630,000 (or 76%) were farmers, the rest priests and their dependants (40,000); the nobility accounted for 2,000, with the poor and other groups numbering 50,000. København had 30,000 inhabitants, the other towns 75,000 in total.

In recent times, the first genuine census of 1769 gave about 800,000 inhabitants in a smaller Denmark without the Skåne provinces, already lost to Sweden. Most towns were fairly small, with only a few having over 3,000 inhabitants (see Table 8 on pp. 154-5). The first accurate census, of 1801, gives 929,000 for the same area, of which 100,000 lived in København and slightly fewer in the remaining towns. The second largest town was Flensborg (in southern Jylland) with about 10,000 inhabitants. The 3 million mark was reached before 1920. Today's population is 5.5 million, with more than 1.5 million living in greater København. In fact, these estimates are becoming increasingly absurd with daily commutes over significant distances becoming a norm for many people, including an increasing number of foreigners.

Periodization

To help clarify the overwhelming amount of data and information on the centuries after AD 1200, the following main phases are identified and discussed in what follows:

Phase IX: A Nation in Flux (the dynamic later Middle Ages up to the Protestant Reformation of 1536: agricultural change, trade, new investments in the towns, including churches; political struggles).

Phase X: Towards Recent Times (the innocent period – in retrospect – up to the great disaster: the loss of the eastern fifth or more of Denmark's population, and as much as a third of its territory, to Sweden in the mid-seventeenth century).

Phase XI: Crisis and Recovery (the crisis and the remarkable recovery of the eighteenth century, based on international trade and the transformation of rural ownership and production at the level of the educated farmer).

Phase XII: A Place in Europe (the new crisis of the Napoleonic Wars, pitting Denmark against Britain, a natural ally, and the German wars, equally pointless but understandable given the rise of nationalism as a basis for government in the face of social challenges).

Phase XIII: Industrial Society (a smaller and resource-empowered Denmark refines agricultural production and promotes exports in tandem with the development of workshop industries; improvement of infrastructure, education and welfare to counter totalitarianism).

Phase XIV: Modernization (the remarkable transformation after World War II, when Denmark passed from being a mainly agricultural society to a country of towns with ever increasing production (paying for social welfare); integration into the western world).

Phase XV: Globalization (the new challenges facing the country in the globalized world of the twenty-first century – fifteen millennia after the arrival of *Homo Sapiens* hunters on the territory that was to become Denmark).

Phase IX. A Nation in Flux (1200-1536)

1200, or perhaps more accurately the mid-thirteenth century, is a convincing archaeological caesura, with Phase IX seeing a new and increased variety in household pottery and consumer goods, including new fashions in clothing (long flowing dresses for men as well as women). A new type of farmstead also appears, with buildings at right angles to one another, like more recent farmsteads (cf. Fig. II.18). There are also changes in the organization of towns, which acquire their own legal codes and special rights, although they still resemble 'digested countryside' in character. Towns may have more than one church, in fact often several, but they had virtually no secular stone buildings.

This is also a period during which many old social structures remained intact. Manor houses were integrated with villages, although a few were built in isolated locations in the countryside for defensive reasons; an example is Næsholm on Sjælland from the end of the thirteenth century, probably a royal estate (La Cour 1961). The

Fig. II.1. St Knud Cathedral, Odense, *c.* 1300. After Johannsen and Smidt 1981.

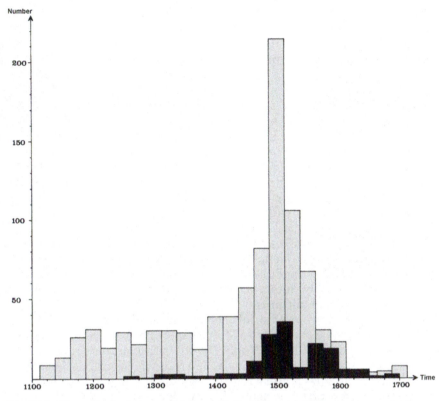

Fig. II.2. Chronological chart of frescos in Danish parish churches; precisely dated frescos in black. The number of Romanesque frescos was no doubt much higher than indicated, but these art works were often destroyed by later building and painting. The peak in around 1500 is a reflection of the intense Gothicization of parish churches. After Wienberg 1993.

widespread system of fortified manor houses as the main economic unit of the elites only emerged with the transformations of the fourteenth century; an example is modest Boringholm in East Jylland (see Topic 6: Boringholm Manor House). There were several reasons for this, including a shortage of man-power resulting from population decline, due in turn to the overexploitation of resources, a general deterioration of the climate, the Black Death in around 1350 and later – a major factor – and demands by other activities (Ulsig 1991). For instance, the 1310s saw crop failures across Europe. It is also assumed that fallow fields became common and that a greater emphasis was placed on cattle rearing, less demanding in terms of labour. Many farms and settlements were abandoned (cf. Table 5 on p. 151).

Some lords still employed stewards on their property to oversee production, but the new system of duties entailed the payment by copyholders of an often modest rent in the form of produce and services. Nevertheless, there was several farmers' revolts. Cheap land prices entailed the expansion and integration of properties, especially among the high nobility in the late fifteenth century. The Danish kings held a monopoly on mints, using coinage as a form of taxation by devaluing the silver content and enforcing a change of currency. They also exacted duties.

The thirteenth century sees the transformation and decline of the Romanesque style and the widespread rise of the Gothic (Fig. II.2). Few country churches were being built (a large number were built in the preceding centuries of Phase VIII). The late Romanesque style – merging with the Gothic – was employed for the new brick monasteries like the Dominican Vor Frue (Our Lady) at Århus (1227+) and the impressive Cistercian Løgumkloster in South Jylland of the same period. The finest Gothic cathedral is St Knud in Odense from 1300 (Fig. II.1), heralding a series of large Gothic town-churches such as St Peter in Malmø in Skåne (1319) and St Peter in Næstved of the close of the fourteenth century. The delightful church belonging to the Brigittine Abbey at Maribo on Lolland (1416) is well preserved. The finest complex, however, is the fully intact Carmelite monastery of St Maria in Helsingør (Elsinore) built in 1430/50 (Fig. II.3).

Church furnishings and burial monuments were often splendid and much has survived from the Late Middle Ages. Perhaps the altar pieces in Århus Cathedral by Bernt Notke (1479), with paintings reminiscent of the Italian Early Renaissance style, and those in Odense Cathedral by Claus Berg (*c.* 1520) – a great realist – should be singled out, but very many others are worthy of note. These include the main altars of the cathedral at Lund (1398) and of the parish church of Boeslunde on

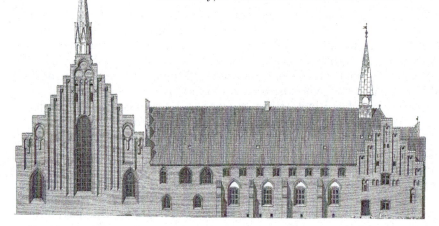

Fig. II.3. St Maria, Helsingør (Elsinore): Carmelite monastery, *c.* 1430/1450+. After Storck 1915.

Sjælland (*c.* 1425). Late medieval churches are also full of fabulous frescos in an almost comic-strip style, including the magnificent and finely executed works by 'The Union Master' in Undløse Church on Sjælland (*c.* 1440); but examples are legion and the number of surviving paintings very high indeed.

The alabaster burial figure of Queen Margrete I in Roskilde Cathedral (*c.* 1420) has an almost classical appearance. Indeed, many fine figurative funerary monuments stem from this period. A wealthy commoner, the Mayor of Ribe Anders Bondesøn (died 1363), had an exquisite monument in brass commissioned in Flanders for himself and his wife Alra. A very elegant gravestone is that of Archbishop Jens Brostrup (died 1497) in Lund Cathedral; a magnificent tombstone by Claus Berg for King Hans (died 1513) can be seen in Odense Cathedral. The latter monument even employs classic Renaissance motifs, some of the earliest in the country. It is perhaps in the arts, and not least in its details, that we can sense a growing individualism.

Fine Gothic castles were built, like the ruined but still impressive Kalø in East Jylland from the beginning of the fourteenth century (1313). A cruciform palace was built by the powerful bishop Lodehat of Roskilde at Gjorslev on Sjælland in 1398, probably inspired by German palaces like Marienburg in East Prussia, headquarters of the German Order, and perhaps with new expansion in the Baltic in mind. The magnificent Glimminghus in Skåne dates to 1499; this is a tall, simple but extremely elegant structure, very well composed from an architectural point of view and with intricate external and internal defences (Fig. II.7). A far more common type of manor house at this period is represented by wooden Boringholm, mentioned above, designed with a lake as a first line of defence.

Throughout the Middle Ages, fishing and the export of enormous amounts of salted herring from specific markets like Skanør-Falsterbo on the Øresund coast in Skåne represented a major source of income for the king (Ersgård 1988); the North German trading cities, like huge Lübeck, had their own crofts at the markets. However, the herring market (though not the large scale fishery) declined during the fifteenth century because of the pronounced growth of the towns, where trade and craft production were the main occupations (cf. Table 6 on p. 152). København and Malmø, both in the Øresund region, underwent a remarkable development, including the building of many private town-houses in brick with stepped gables (like contemporary churches), such as Brahe House at Ystad in Skåne (Fig. II.5). Even apartment houses were made of brick; an example is the long structure built by Mayor Thuesen of Næstved town on Sjælland (Fig. II.6).

In this period, wide cog ships with substantial cargo capacity plied the waves and made Denmark rich and powerful after the crises and transformations of the fourteenth century, including the Black Death.

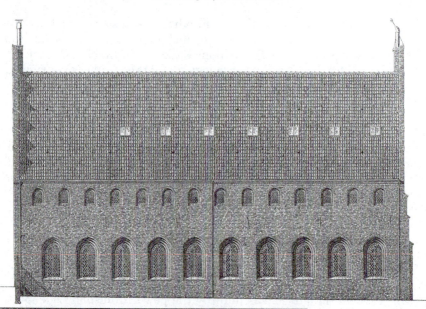

Fig. II.4. Holy Spirit monastery, København 1469+; (*left*) the hospital wing during restoration. After Storck 1911; *Opmålinger*.

Fig. II.5. Town mansion belonging to the noble Brahe family, Ystad, Skåne (1480s). Gothic in style; the entrance (not shown) displays Italian Early Renaissance elements. The cousin of the builder was lady-in-waiting to the Danish queen and accompanied her to through Italy to Rome. Photo: Author.

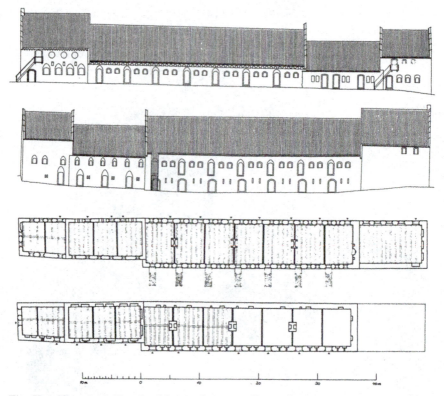

Fig. II.6. Thuesen's Booths, Næstved, 1484+. Part of an apartment estate from the Late Middle Ages. After Høyer 1988.

For about a decade in the crisis-ridden early fourteenth century the country was pawned to raise money. Only military resistance saved the kingdom, which entered a new period of prosperity under King Valdemar IV 'Day-Again' (1340-75).

In 1397, the Nordic 'Kalmar' Union was born under Danish leadership and specifically that of Valdemar IV's daughter Margrete I (died 1412). Denmark had acquired Norway and the North Atlantic nations, and managed to take over Sweden (and with it Finland as well). Northern Estland (Estonia) was sold to raise money, while Gotland was conquered in 1361 (Westholm 2007). Denmark succeeded in keeping the Germans at bay in the Baltic and the English in the North Atlantic. Nonetheless, the Norsemen of Greenland vanished in around AD 1450 – possibly unbeknownst to the Danish king – while Iceland resisted into modern times.

This is also a century of new and wide-ranging changes in pottery and household consumption, with new types of tableware and a new diversity in eating habits. Other changes include consumer habits, such as new fashions in clothing. Men now wear short jackets and trousers;

Fig. II.7. Glimmingehus, Skåne, 1499, probably by Adam von Düren. After Holm et al. 1894.

women's clothes also become rather revealing. By 1500 extravagance and bright colours are dominant. Baggy sleeves and short coats become fashionable for men, who also wear broad-brimmed hats. Women wear tall pointed hats, and fur and silk are widely used. The fashion in shoes also changes. Clearly life must have taken a turn for the better, not least among the nobility and the bourgeois elites.

The late fifteenth century saw the advent of the large caravel ship. It also witnessed a more widespread use of gunpowder for cannon, as well as professional and often mercenary infantry armies. A permanent naval force was established in around 1500. The fortified shipyard of Engelsborg (Engberg and Frandsen 2006) was constructed on a small island off Lolland (Fig. II.8): the enemy was clearly the large trading city of Lübeck, which even attacked København in the early fifteenth century in response to the new Øresund Dues. Lübeck's old blocking ships – an attempt to put a stop to maritime traffic and trade – were recently found during excavations for the new opera house in København.

Permission to open the first Danish university was granted by the Pope in 1475, at a time when many Danes studied abroad (about twenty-five each year at the University of Rostock alone). The first Danish printed book dates to 1482. But these changes went deeper; on the one hand we note a popular engagement in religion (as often occurs in periods of change), on the other a growing rebellion against the church. Protestantism emerged, taking a particularly early hold in affluent Malmø across the Øresund from København.

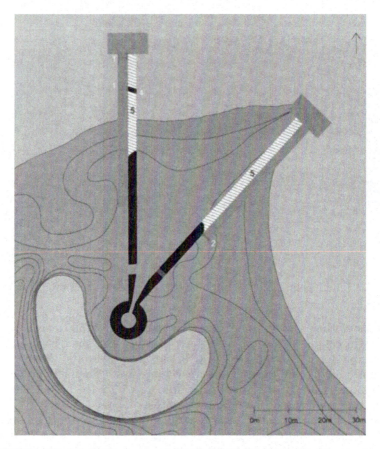

Fig. II.8. Fortified Engelsborg naval ship yard, Lolland, 1509+. The yard consists of two walls meeting in a heavy tower; ships were constructed between
the walls, then launched into the sea. After Engberg and Frandsen 2006. 1-2 =
careening area; 4-5 = extensions of flanking walls.

The century before the Protestant Reformation of 1536 saw enormous
investments in the modernization of parish churches, which were
significantly enlarged and endowed with Gothic vaults, large pointed-
arched windows, brick towers, stepped gables and not least new frescos
(see Fig. II.2). New monasteries were built, mostly in the towns,
alongside other institutions such as hospitals (see Figs II.3-4).
Architectural inspiration came from North Germany, in particular the
great trading town of Lübeck. The Protestant Reformation thus
coincides with wealth, great religious and social engagement, and
cultural change. It also took place only a few years after Columbus'
voyages and was no doubt conditioned by the frightening new world
opened up by European expansion across the Seven Seas.

Opposition to the Catholic Church was so strong that the Gothic style died out in the process. Renaissance-style elements are virtually unknown in the Catholic period, but this was the idiom chosen to express the new state of affairs. Even the old Romanesque style gained new appreciation, as indicated by the 1508 proposal advanced by King Hans (reign: 1481-1513) to restore the Cathedral of Lund rather than adding new buildings in the Gothic style (Nielsen 1987, 30).

On an aesthetic level, the Gothic style is vertical and unfettered in structure and character, whilst the Renaissance style is horizontal, repetitive and bound – perhaps reflecting the different conception of the divine as opposed to the secular world, or secular society. Buildings are in fact ideologically loaded and expressive of open-ended choices, a fact naturally exploited by patrons.

Phase X. Towards Recent Times (1536-1660)

Political and social developments around and after 1500 were also dramatic. The Nordic Union of 1397 led to disputes and wars between Denmark and Sweden on several occasions, struggles which in the seventeenh century almost cost Denmark its status as an independent nation. The execution in 1520 of much of the Swedish elite in Stockholm, for which King Christian II (1513-23), popular among the bourgeoisie and in particular the merchants, was held responsible effectively put an end to the Nordic Union. King Christian II was later dethroned and replaced by one of his father's brothers, Frederik I (1523-33). From his exile he tried to recapture Denmark with the support of his brother-in-law, the German Emperor, but was caught and imprisoned for the rest of his life. He died in 1559.

Conflicts of interest even led to civil war (1534-36) and farmers' rebellions, which were crushed. Eventually the Lutheran Christian III (1534-59), son of Frederik I, was elected king; in 1536 he ordered that Protestantism be the creed of all Denmark. Acceptance of the new doctrines was generalized and undisputed. Religious antagonism never represented a genuine threat to the country's social fabric (much as in the 960s when Christianity was generally accepted). Many priests embraced Lutheranism and monks were often permitted to remain in their monasteries till they died. Nevertheless, many abbeys and even churches, in particular in the towns, were demolished during this process, in accordance with the dictum 'one parish – one church'. The resulting materials were reused to construct secular buildings. Christian III – like a latter day King Svend (died 1014) – secured the kingdom by building a series of heavily fortified castles with round corner bastions for cannon batteries.

Vast church properties in the form of land and buildings were confiscated. The drastic decrease in the economic power of the Church

71

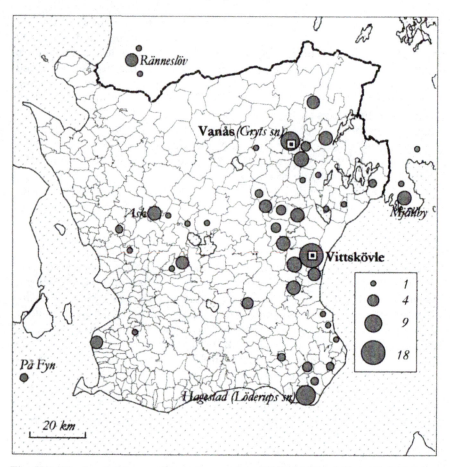

Fig. II.9. The landed possessions of a member of the high nobility, Niels Brahe, owner of the manor houses of Vanås and Vittskövle (Vidskøvle) and of some 200 farmsteads in Skåne (the dots), *c.* 1525. After Olsson et al. 2006.

after the Protestant Reformation gave the king and the nobility new room for manoeuvre and allowed them to invest in the splendid Renaissance palaces and manor houses that still dot the Danish landscape. These include Rosenholm of 1559 with its exquisite 'Pirkentavl' Pavilion or Voergård of 1578 with its magnificent gateway, both in Jylland; Hesselagergård of 1538+, with 'Italian' gables, and elegant Egeskov of 1554, both on Fyn; or, for example, Borreby of 1556, Lystrup of 1579 and huge Vallø of 1581, all on Sjælland; Vidskøvle of 1553 – ironically, the largest manor house in Sweden today – and fine Svendstrup of 1596, also in Skåne (cf. Fig. II.9).

The double Danish-German province of Slesvig-Holstein as always represented a problem – and an opportunity. However, the fact that both

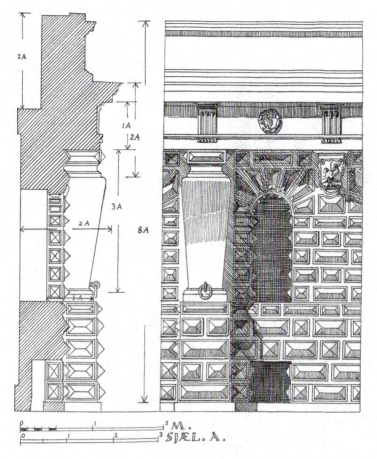

Fig. II.10. Kronborg Palace: (*above*) details of 1574+; (*below*) Dark Gate of 1577 by Harmen Gertsen. After Wanscher 1939 and Norn 1954.

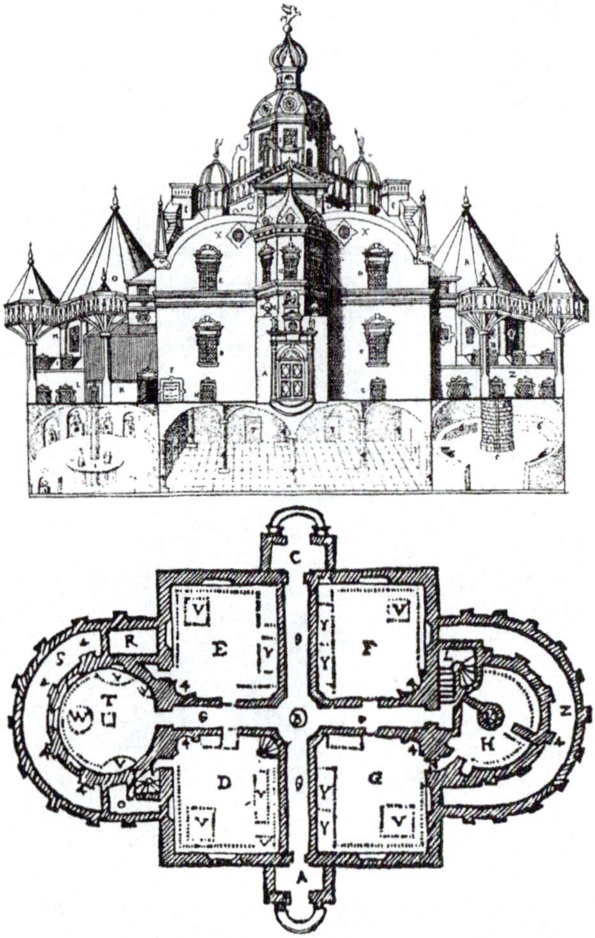

Fig. II.11. Tycho
Brahe's Uranieborg
Observatory, Island of
Hven in Øresund.
After Randsborg 2004.

Frederik I and Christian III were dukes of Slesvig-Holstein before they became kings of Denmark helped keep the province as part of the kingdom. A division might have been possible in the Late Middle Ages, but now Denmark both gained (by controlling an important border region and gateway to the continent) and lost (by being stuck with a national problem only 'resolved' with the German conquest of the whole province in 1864 and North Slesvig's return to Denmark in 1920).

The reign of King Frederik II (1559-88) benefited from stable conditions and even modest conquests like that of the free Frisians in Dithmarschen and the island of Øsel (in Estland/Estonia); a seven-year war with Sweden from 1563-70 (the Danish side dreaming of reestablishing the Nordic Union), was costly but changed little. In fact, the Nordic Union had probably increased the rivalry between

Denmark and Sweden rather than putting these nations at peace with each other.

Denmark's architectural accomplishments were of enduring importance. In 1563 the architect Peter de Dunker adorned the naval anchor forge (now Holmen's Church) with an elegant gable in Italian Renaissance style, virtually rising out of the waters; doubtless one of the most modern structures in northern Europe at this time. It was also the first sight to greet anyone leaving København Castle. At Helsingør (Elsinore) on Sjælland, Frederik II transformed the late medieval Krogen ('corner') Castle into the truly magnificent Kronborg Palace of the 1570s (Fig. II.10). Kronborg is northern Europe's best-known Renaissance castle and perhaps its finest; it is rivalled only by beautiful Frederiksborg Castle at Hillerød on Sjælland, rebuilt in the early seventeenth century by Frederik II's son, King Christian IV. Kronborg was also the first castle in Denmark to have angular or 'Dutch' bastions, marking the beginning of a long period of scientific siege warfare and countermeasures.

Krogen and Kronborg presided over the collection of the Øresund dues for passage into and out of the Baltic. These dues were an extremely important source of income for the Danish crown and were only abolished in the mid-1800s, when the nations of the world paid a one-off compensation. Shakespeare even seems to have contemplated Kronborg in his *Hamlet* of *c.* 1600. The play is actually an indirect expression of English fears regarding the sudden death (after a 'bad drink') in April 1588 of a valued Protestant ally, King Frederik II, and his widow's attempt to marry his brother. Their son, Christian IV – 'Hamlet' – (born in 1577) was only a child at the time. The attack by the Spanish Armada on England in 1588 immediately followed Frederik II's death.

King Christian IV (reign 1588-1648) is particularly fondly remembered by the Danes, although the later years of his reign saw a new decline leading to the Swedish conquest of the provinces to the east of Øresund (in 1658) and in particular Skåne, an extremely valuable and densely populated part of the country. Christian IV's fine palaces and churches, many in København and its environs, are much loved (Fig. II.12).

To choose but one from the long list of Christian IV's architectural accomplishments is difficult, but perhaps the lovely gateway of the first Rosenborg Palace in København (of 1606+) should take pride of place (Randsborg 2004) (see Topic 7: Rosenborg Gateway). It was probably built to a design by Inigo Jones, one of King Christian's many artist servants – making the court one of Europe's most prominent in its heyday. Christian's sister was Queen Anne of Scotland and England. Another much loved building is Rundetårn ('Round Tower') in København (of 1637), actually a staircase tower and astronomical observation platform connected to a church housing the university

Fig. II.12. Prospect of København by J. Dircksen of 1611. After Randsborg 2004.

library in the huge space above the nave: the 'staircase' itself forms a large helix that could even accommodate carriages (the Russian Tsar Peter the Great once drove to the top of the tower).

The numerous building activities of the Renaissance and later – some impressive even on a European level – were very expensive for the crown and the nobility. The higher bourgeoisie – mainly wealthy merchants – also invested in buildings; an example is Jens Bang and his huge town mansion of 1624 in Ålborg, North Jylland, surpassing any such building in København.

To prepare Denmark for the future and especially for Swedish attacks, an impressive naval dockyard (1598) was built at København, alongside a series of fortresses and even planned fortified towns throughout the realm. But money was limited, military visions restricted (despite their high ambitions) and a standing army was never formed, although the navy was well equipped. King Christian IV took a

particular interest in Norway (including safeguarding the country from Swedish attacks in the north). On the commercial side, he acquired lands in India and at home attempted to establish a silk factory in København. A fine department store, 'Børsen' (the stock exchange), with its elegant spire of twisted dragons' tails, was built next to the castle but did not meet with much success; the building nevertheless housed Denmark's first public post office. The king even took an interest in orphaned children, who were put to work in the hope of giving them an education – and bolstering production (Olsen 1978).

On the intellectual front, København University was re-established as a Protestant institution in 1537, but scientific and other academic accomplishments were still largely the province of individuals such as the astronomer Tycho Brahe (1546-1601), a member of the high nobility and a master of empiricism, who in 1572 observed a new star and thus proved that the universe is not as it was established at the Creation. Brahe also built impressive observatories, including the 'Palladian' Uranieborg of 1576 on the island of Hven in the Øresund (Fig. II.11).

Fig. II.13. Rasmus Svendsen's country school of 1633, Faxe, Sjælland. Photo: Author.

Another prominent scholar was the physician and antiquarian Ole Worm (1588-1654), who not only established a large museum (whose collections he also published) but also collected antiquarian information parish by parish throughout Denmark and Norway: an extremely comprehensive and systematic work that truly revolutionized ways of approaching the past (Worm 1655; cf. Worm 1643-51) (Randsborg 1994) (Fig. II.14).

Apart from the revenues obtained through dues and trade, agriculture remained the mainstay of the economy. In a lovely wood-cut showing Lejre Village on Sjælland, published by Ole Worm in 1643, we see a number of ancient monuments including a mound and ship-settings. Six four-wing farmsteads of identical size and some smaller buildings occupy the foreground. In fact, in the late seventeenth century there were six farms and a smallholding at Lejre, all with the same amount of land in the village's various fields. Farms of equal size within cooperative villages are a characteristic feature of this period. Indeed, Renaissance agriculture was as effective as we might deduce from the settlements and their structures. It is only in retrospect that this type of organization was to trade individual effectiveness for collaboration and egalitarianism.

The actual owners resided elsewhere, typically in their manor houses, which had been run since the Late Middle Ages as fairly efficient independent units, supported by work from dependent copyholders.

Fig. II.14. Ole Worms's Museum, mid-seventeenth century. After Worm 1655.

Usually, manor houses were built in the borderlands between parishes, often surrounded by forest. Wealthy noblemen had widespread possessions. Thus Niels Brahe of Vidskøvle and Vandås in Skåne owned about 200 farms in 1529, most of which in the same province, when he was executed for treason for supporting Christian II against King Frederik I (Olsson, Skansjö and Sundberg 2006) (see Fig. II.9).

Phase XI. Crisis and Recovery (1660-1800)

Unfortunately, Christian IV continued Denmark's rivalry with Sweden in another costly and unsuccessful war, the Kalmar War of 1611-13 (see Topic 8: Wars with Sweden). More dangerous still was his attempt to become the protector of German Protestantism in opposition to the Catholic German Emperor. A decisive battle at Lutter am Barenberge south of Hannover in 1627 led to the Catholic occupation of Jylland (a wounded King Christian IV barely escaped the battle). Denmark received rather mild peace terms, whilst Sweden continued to expand; at Lützen near Leipzig in 1632 the Swedish-led Protestant forces won a decisive battle against the Catholic armies at the cost of King Gustaf Adolf's life. The so-called Thirty Years War, in which Sweden also participated, dragged on in Central Europe until 1648. In 1643 Swedish forces suddenly marched into Jylland from the south and into Skåne from Sweden. King Christian IV returned on board ship in the navy at the age of 67 and was again wounded in battle. In 1645, Denmark was forced to cede Halland, along with Jemtland and Herjedalen in Norway, for 30 years. Gotland and Øsel in the Baltic were also lost. The balance of power in Scandinavia was tipping towards Sweden.

In 1657 Denmark, now ruled by King Frederik III (1648-70), naively declared war on Sweden. The Swedish army on the continent made peace with its enemies, marched into Jylland and during the very cold winter months of 1658 crossed over the ice to the Danish islands, normally protected by the sea and the strong Danish navy (see Fig. III.23). This was a military gamble; the Swedish army could easily have ended up on the bottom of the Bælts. At the Peace of Roskilde, Denmark was forced to give up all its eastern provinces in addition to Bohus and Trondhjem in Norway, thus cutting the latter in two. The Dukes of Slesvig-Holstein became virtual allies of Sweden. Later in 1658, the Swedish King Karl Gustaf decided to capture all of Denmark, landing at Korsør on Sjælland and laying siege to København. The largest Swedish fortification ever – Karlstad – was built on a large hill just outside København (see Fig. III.24). However, the capital received Dutch support and a massive Swedish attack in 1659 failed completely. After a new peace in 1660, Trondhjem and Bornholm returned to the Danish crown. However, the population of the provinces lost to Sweden, especially Skåne, was terrorized and guerrilla warfare continued into the eighteenth century. To 'Free Denmark' the Roskilde Peace still represents a trauma. Worst of all. perhaps, Denmark turned its back on Skåne, letting down the captured Danes. Books in Danish were banned in Skåne until well into the nineteenth century.

A new war with Sweden, the Skåne War; followed in 1675-79. Denmark actually reconquered most of its lost provinces and won some crucial battles, not least at sea, but failed to prevail at the negotiating table (Einarsson 2001). The same was true during the Great Nordic War of 1700-20. The only benefit for Denmark was that the dukes of Slesvig-Holstein remained subject to the Danish crown and that Sweden (and Finland) became weaker after 1720 following losses to Russia.

The war also had consequences for the Danish nobility, traditionally the country's backbone – controlling much of its wealth, exempt from paying taxes, commanders of the armed forces and members of the council of the kingdom with the right to elect the king and even to limit his powers. During the siege of København the balance of power shifted and the wealthy bourgeoisie gained new influence, in particular since they had financed the war against securities in crown lands. In fact, an absolute monarchy was introduced in 1660, with the king at the head of a new council of professional politicians (a *de facto* government).

Ministries employing civil servants were introduced, a new high court was established and a new law code for the entire country issued. Punishments were severe, at least according to the law (and not least for lèse-majesté). A comparison of penalties for the same crimes from the Middle Ages to the present is a very interesting and socially instructive exercise (see Table 7 on p. 153). Of particular importance is the establishment of functional and non-corrupt legal and administrative institutions with the advent of the absolute monarchy, a precondition for the introduction of democracy some 175 years later.

After 1720, Denmark and Norway remained at peace till 1801. During this period, international and domestic trade flourished. Scientific journeys included Carsten Niebuhr's expedition to the Near East (1761-7). At the end of the nineteenth century, the Danish merchant fleet was the second largest in the world (after that of Great Britain). Denmark held its Indian possessions from 1620 to 1845/69. The first Indian university (and museum) was founded by Denmark in Calcutta. Denmark started to colonize St Thomas in the Caribbean in 1666 as the first of the Virgin Islands ruled by Denmark until World War I (1917). Various West African possessions (Danish until 1850), mainly in Ghana, were initially conquered from Sweden in 1658: the only compensation for the great loss of the eastern provinces.

In the eighteenth century, Danes actively participated in the so-called 'triangular trade' bringing European goods such as firearms, alcohol and fabric to Africa, African slaves as a work force to the Caribbean and Caribbean luxury products to Europe. Denmark alone exported some 50,000 slaves from Africa. However, it was also the first country to abolish the slave-trade (in 1791, effective from 1792), even establishing the first European plantation in sub-Saharan Africa in the 1780s. The idea was to avoid the trade in human beings by producing 'Caribbean' goods in Africa (the project failed). Norway – the Danish equivalent of Scotland – became increasingly important in economic terms during the eighteenth century, in particular for iron and other industries, alongside traditional shipping, fishing and other trades. A university was founded in 1811. With Finland gradually falling to Russia (the country became independent only after World War I), Sweden aimed to conquer Norway. A strong Danish navy was the main guarantee of keeping Norway under Danish rule.

The wars of the mid-seventeenth century virtually put a stop to prestigious building projects in Denmark. Yet soon after 1660 a new series of buildings in the classicizing architectural idiom of the absolutist monarchy – the Baroque – were erected, especially in København, the kingdom's imperial capital. The new and impenetrable corner fortress 'Kastellet' (the Fortress) has simple well-designed gateways. Facing København Castle, a huge administrative building for cannon, archives and the king's Art Chamber was built in 1665; its design, too, is plain but elegant. New churches include Vor Frelser (Our

Fig. II.15. Vor Frelser (Our
Saviour) Church, København, by
L. van Haven, 1681+. After L. de
Thurah 1746-49.

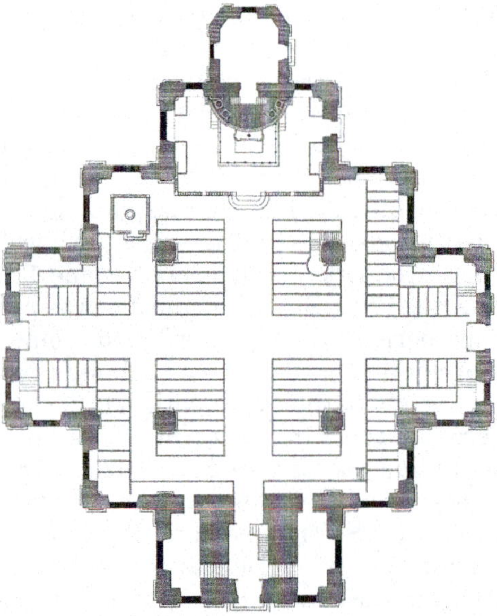

Saviour) of 1681+ in København – built after the Skåne War – a masterpiece of scientific design (Fig. II.15).

This fondness for building was hard on older structures. To give but one example, the early fourteenth-century Kalø Castle ended up as building materials for a fine Baroque palace of 1672+ in København (Charlottenborg, now the Academy of Arts). The magnificent first Christiansborg Palace of 1733+, a veritable Versailles, replaced old København Castle. Frederiksberg Palace of 1699+, like Versailles located immediately outside the city, had the requisite grand park. Fredensborg Palace on Sjælland of 1719 is also situated in a fine park, while the elegant Eremitage Palace of 1734 is a tall royal hunting lodge in an extensive forest near København. Baroque manor houses include the fine København mansion of Admiral Niels Juel (1683) – hero of the Skåne War – serene Clausholm in Jylland (1692) and elegant Nysø on Sjælland (1671), built by one of the new high-level civil servants of the absolute monarchy. Finally, it is worth mentioning the imposing and elegant Amalienborg complex with its four identical palaces of 1750 (now the Royal Palace) in København. The complex is home to one of Europe's finest equestrian statues: King Frederik V (1746-66) dressed as a Roman emperor, the last of such royal portraits. From this time onwards the monarch was portrayed in military uniform or black dress – the king symbolically becoming a member of the ever more powerful bourgeoisie: a very interesting development with implications for the future and even for the present.

The Danish love of music was always strong, as demonstrated by Christian IV's investments in international court musicians. The Danish Diderik (or Dietrich) Hansen Buxtehude (1637-1707) composed some of Europe's finest Baroque music, mainly for the organ. He was J.S. Bach's teacher and was admired by G.F. Händel. W.A. Mozart's widow Constanze married a Dane, settled in København and helped to promote musical life at the Royal Theatre.

The eighteenth century was an age of both rationalism and refinement, stressing education and information as well as entertainment. A public Royal Theatre did not open till 1748, but private theatres are older. The historian Ludvig Holberg (1684-1754), Norwegian by birth but resident in Denmark from the age of 18, was a child of the Enlightenment. He was also a truly great writer, best known today for his humorous and socially perceptive plays, which are still performed. They include *Erasmus Montanus* (*Rasmus Berg*) of 1723 about a farmer's son who, having modernized his name, returns to his home village from the University at København claiming that the earth is 'round'.

What is interesting is that the young man in the play was able to attend university at all. This can be explained by the country schools: 241 standardized royal schools for children, both boys and girls, from the age of five until their confirmation, were established across the country in 1721. Lessons took place from 7-11 am and 2-6 pm in summer and from 8-12 am and 2-4 pm in winter; beating the children was prohibited. In fact, schools for commoners are also known in earlier periods, like that at Faxe on Sjælland, founded in 1634 with financial support from a nephew of Tycho Brahe (II.13). Latin schools (secondary schools) were already established in the cities and towns by the Middle Ages, but were only for boys. The nobility and wealthy commoners could afford private teachers for their children.

Among the other social institutions of the period is the elegant Frederik's Hospital in København of 1752, where poor people received free care. Perhaps even more important is the nearby Royal Maternity Hospital of 1750 where women paid according to their means for superb hygienic rooms and professional care. These institutions lowered the number of deaths in childbirth which had plagued women since the Stone Age with resulting low life expectancy and a limited social life. Women nonetheless lived rather protected lives as demonstrated by the wounds recorded on skeletons through history (Grimm 1977): in the Palaeolithic both sexes endured the same physical hardships; by the Iron Age men bore 90% of the wounds – evidence of an increasing division of labour with men facing far more hazards.

The search for alternatives to the absolute monarchy intensified in the late eighteenth century, with a new interest in commoners and their deeds, and a fascination for the distant past (a possible source of inspiration). A remarkable sculpture park was opened at the royal castle of Jægerspris on Sjælland in 1776+, centred on two Neolithic passage graves. The memorials hailed the 'bourgeois' deeds of the mainly non-noble citizens of Denmark and Norway. The artistic language employed by J. Wiedewelt (1731-1802) was highly original, expressing an almost post-modernist interpretation of classical antiquity, supposed to be 'Nordic'. The sponsor – the equivalent of Denmark's Prime Minister – himself translated and published Cicero's *Republic*. The interest in classical antiquity as a model for society (Nordic prehistory was scarcely known at the time) found particular expression in the new Neoclassicist language of architecture with its roots in Britain where the Baroque style of the absolute monarchies was virtually absent. With France being seen as the main enemy, classicizing Palladianism in continuation of Inigo Jones was the major architectural style of this period in Britain (exemplified by the works of C. Wren (1632-1723), including St Paul's Cathedral in London of 1675+).

Some of the earliest Neoclassical structures on the continent are in fact Danish and include Bernstorff Castle of 1759 near København and Marienlyst Palace, also of 1759, at Helsingør on Sjælland, with a Renaissance pavilion of 1588 as its core (Randsborg 1992; 2004). The much-admired Petit Trianon at Versailles was only begun three years

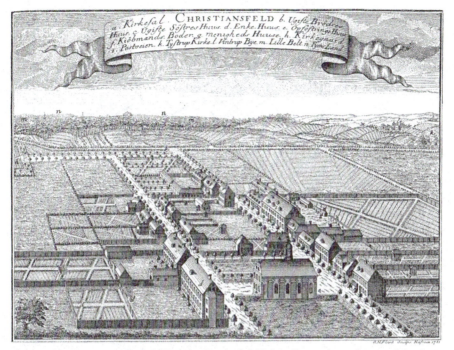

Fig. II.16. Christiansfeld, Jylland: planned religiously motivated township (by Herrnhuts) of 1771. After Pontoppidan 1763-81.

later. Among the manor houses of this period are elegant Hagenskov (Frederiksgave) of 1774 on Fyn and Dronninggård on Sjælland of 1782, the summer home of the great merchant F. de Coninck, owner of up to 60 ships, in addition to many chartered vessels – a genuine eighteenth-century Mærsk Line. De Coninck went bankrupt in the wake of the English attacks on København in 1801 and 1807 and the cessation of Denmark's high sea trade during the Napoleonic Wars. A religious community even founded a planned settlement, Christiansfeld: adopting the idiom of modesty and simplicity familiar to us from the material culture of the Shakers in the USA and similar groups (Fig. II.16).

More important for Denmark's social fabric was the transformation of rural society in the late eighteenth century in an attempt to increase production. The structure of villages remained identical to that described above, with farmers usually paying rent to noble (and other) owners and tilling the land collectively. This was because, in order to ensure fairness, land was distributed in narrow strips across the various fields belonging to the village (Fig. II.17). The idea of creating a class of independent farmers tilling their own land as they wished and living in fine well-built structures began to gain ground (Fig. II.18). The whole country was mapped in great detail and the land redistributed. Forests

85

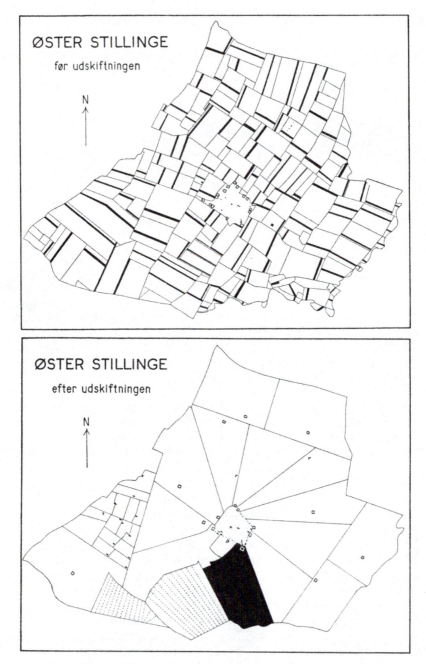

Fig. II.17. Øster Stillinge, Sjælland: ownership of land by one farm in a village, before (*above*) and after (*below*) regulation at the close of the eighteenth century. After Nielsen et al. 1958.

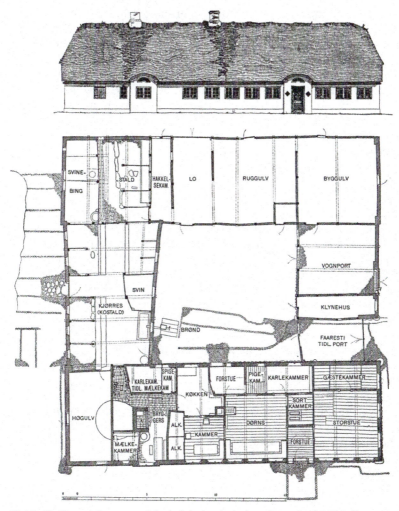

Fig. II.18. Ordinary farmstead in brick (and timber frame) of 1803: Lønnestak, West Jylland. After Jespersen 1947. *Høgulv* = hay floor (room); *Mælkekammer* = milk chamber (storage); *Karlekam. tidl. mælkekam.* = male servants' room, formerly a milk chamber; *Spisekammer* = foods (refined) chamber (storage); *Bryggers* = 'brewery' = second kitchen (baking, brewing, washing); *Alk.* = alcove (bedstead); *Køkken* = kitchen (for cooking); *Kammer* = chamber; *Forstue* = entrance-hall; *Pigekam.* = female servants' room; *dørns* = sitting room (heated); *Karlekammer* = male servants' room; *Dørns* = sitting room (heated); *Sort kammer* = 'black chamber' (no real window; storage); *Gæstekammer* = guest room; *Storstue* = hall (unheated); *Kjørres* (kostald) = cow stable; *Svin* = pig; *Svinebing* = pigsty; *Stald* = stable (horses); *Hakkelseskam.* = cut fodder (for animals) chamber; *Lo* = barn; *Ruggulv* = 'rye floor' (threshing and storage); *Byggulv* = 'barley floor' (threshing and storage); *Vognport* = wagon house; *Klynehus* = peat house (fuel storage); *Fåresti tidl. port* = sheep-pen, ex.-gateway; *Brønd* = well.

were walled – a massive task – to keep grazing animals out and promote scientific forestry. Some farmsteads remained inside villages but many moved out into the fields, creating today's complex filled-in rural landscape, although this settlement pattern is largely an illusion: land is now concentrated in fewer and fewer hands with the use of machinery and automated stables. The revolution in around 1800 was also led from the top and included various other decrees, in particular the abolition of adscription that had tied many farmers to their land since the Late Middle Ages, in later times partly with an eye to enrolment in the militias (the field army was professional).

A bizarre but interesting episode occurred when the doctor attending the mentally ill King Christian VII (1766-1808), J.F. Struensee (1737-72), began to issue decrees in the absolute monarch's name. His orders were children of an age of radical enlightenment – all would meet with approval today – and included employment according to qualifications, simplification of the bureaucracy, press freedom, free trade, improvement of schools and care for the poor, and even minor matters including a state lottery and request for house numbers – but they aroused massive opposition among the elites and others. Struensee was executed. A particular problem was his relationship with the young English-born Queen Caroline Mathilde (1751-75), who bore his child Louise Augusta; her own daughter later married King Christian VIII (reign 1839-48). Gossip about important people is nothing new.

Phase XII. A Place in Europe (1800-1864)

In the eighteenth century Denmark benefited greatly from its overseas trade, not least as a neutral power catering to all sides during the Napoleonic Wars, with warships often escorting merchant vessels: so-called 'armed neutrality'. Denmark protected its merchantmen everywhere; Tripoli in Libya, for instance, was attacked in 1797 to free captured Danish sailors. An alliance of neutral powers was formed, but Britain chose to strike Denmark (see Topic 9: Battles with England), attacking København in the spring of 1801. To prevent bombard ships from getting too close to the capital, a line of old ships-of-the-line and other vessels was formed (the active fleet was not ready after the winter).

On board the *Elephant*, Admiral Horatio Nelson, hero of the Nile, assaulted the Danish line – outnumbered two to one – south of the Trekroner sea fortress in a six-hour battle leaving (roughly) 500 dead and 550 wounded on the Danish side (higher numbers are claimed) and 300 dead and 650 wounded on the British side (Feldbæk 1985). Nelson threatened to set fire to the captured Danish ships (with the prisoners still on board), thus forcing the Danes to end hostilities. Trekroner and the Danish line to the north were intact, but were unable to prevent the bombardment of København. The political outcome was an armistice followed by Denmark's withdrawal from its position as a neutral power. Incidentally, the notorious Commander William Bligh of *Bounty* fame also fought at København, demanding a letter from Nelson stating that he had acquitted himself well.

In 1805 Nelson crushed the French-Spanish fleet at Trafalgar, making the Danish fleet the largest on the continent and a potential means for Napoleon to invade England. In the summer of 1807 England stood alone and was threatened by blockade; it demanded the surrender of the Danish fleet. Virtually all of the Danish army was deployed on the southern border to prevent an attack by Napoleon. The militias on Sjælland were crushed by Wellington, later the victor at Waterloo; a hopeless ten-hour encounter at Køge ('Clog Battle') between seasoned British soldiers and Danish farmers cost 150 British casualties but more than twice as many Danish victims (Hedegaard 1970). Other British troops laid siege to København and started a fire missile bombardment that terrorized the capital into accepting British demands: civilian casualties were heavy. The capture of the navy – more than 37 warships – put an end to the double monarchy, although this was followed by several years of war against Britain and other powers, including Sweden, Prussia and Russia. Norway was ceded to Sweden in 1815 (a declaration of independence was ignored). However, Greenland, Iceland and the Faroe Islands remained under Danish rule as København had been the protector of the North Atlantic lands since the fourteenth century. Even before the end of the Napoleonic Wars, Denmark had gone bankrupt.

The events which followed were truly remarkable. Denmark was now a small and impoverished country, which had difficulties recovering from the crisis even with a surplus of agricultural products after the end of the Napoleonic Wars (food prices were falling). Yet its social fabric was strong, and the fact that the kingdom was now a nation state seems to have released new energies among the well-educated bourgeois elites, in particular in København. Over 20% of the population lived in towns, most of them in the capital (see Tables 8-9 on pp. 154-5). Romanticism celebrated both the distant past and contemporary life and led to a remarkably rich phase in Danish literature and the arts.

World-famous authors such as Hans Christian Andersen (1805-75) and the philosopher Søren Kierkegaard (1813-55), the brilliant Empire architect C.F. Hansen (1756-1845) and Golden Age painters such as C.W. Eckersberg (1783-1853) and the calm yet intense C.S. Købke (1810-48) paved the way for later developments; Købke's paintings can be seen at the National Gallery in London as well as in Edinburgh. The Empire style is a late Romanized version of Neoclassicism; its *quasi-*Bauhaus simplicity reappears on a different level in painting and even in the tales of H.C. Andersen. B. Thorvaldsen (1770-1844), an important and internationally orientated Neoclassicist sculptor, lived in Rome for many years and represented an important link with the eighteenth century. At the Royal Theatre, A. August Bournonville (1805-79) established a famous ballet company and school still performing to international applause. In the sciences, H.C. Ørsted (1777-1851), the discoverer of electromagnetism – a prerequisite for the petrol engine – and C.J. Thomsen (1788-1865), father of the Danish National Museum (of 1807) and inventor of the Three-Period System in archaeological chronology (the Stone, Bronze and Iron Ages), are both world-renowned.

Interestingly, these figures took little intellectual interest in contemporary life, nor did they have a vision for the future. Denmark's first steam engines actually date to as early as the close of the eighteenth century and the first railways to the 1840s. Only Hans Christian Andersen appears to have noticed: 'Yes, in a thousand years they will fly through the air on wings of steam across the oceans! The young citizens of America will visit old Europe' (the opening of the story 'In a Thousand Years', 1853).

Politically, this period sees the first democratic institutions in the form of small parliaments in different parts of the kingdom, founded in 1831 with members from all social groups except the poor. These parliaments became hotbeds of debate on nationalist issues – such as the future of Slesvig – and cautious evaluations of the declining absolute monarchy. Unfortunately, this was followed not only by democratic reform but also by new wars, this time with Germany, in connection with nationalist struggles in Europe (see Topic 10: At War with Germany).

The First Slesvig War (1848-50) began with a demand for freedom from the Danish crown on the part of the German Slesvig-Holsteiners and by a demand for democracy on the part of the Danish population. The Danish position was that Slesvig – the Danish part of the Duchy – should remain part of the kingdom of Denmark, whilst German Holstein was free to leave. The German response was to form a Slesvig-Holstein government and army, resisted by Denmark. Denmark easily won the initial encounters, but Prussia intervened. In the face of superior enemy forces, the Danish army withdrew to fortified positions in Jylland (while the navy blockaded German harbours). A successful sortie was made from the town of Fredericia in 1849. Under pressure from Russia, Prussia then withdrew its forces. The Slesvig-Holstein army was defeated in Scandinavia's largest ever land-battle at Isted in 1850. After the war, things continued much as before, though nationalist sentiments grew stronger, especially in Germany.

Danish politicians still dreamed of Slesvig as an integral part of a democratic Denmark (the democratic constitution was signed during the war). In 1863, on the death of King Frederik VII (reign: 1848-63), a new constitution linking Slesvig more closely to Denmark was signed and war predictably commenced with Prussia (led by Bismarck) and the

Austro-Hungarian empire, the major powers supporting the German Slesvig-Holsteiners.

The Danish army was in position at the old but improved Danevirke walls in South Slesvig (cf. Fig. I.17), but the winter ice, allowing for an attack on its unprotected right flank, forced the army to withdraw to a fortified position at Dybbøl further north. Dybbøl was stormed in April 1864 with horrific losses on the Danish side, outnumbered three to one. Early withdrawal to the island of Als would have kept the Danish army in Slesvig during the final negotiations. Virtually all of Slesvig had now been lost. The only Danish victories were at sea, thanks to the stronger Danish navy. At that time, southern Slesvig was fairly Germanized but it is possible that a border could have been drawn south of Flensborg town (and north of Slesvig City) with British and French support; no doubt this would have been the case before the war. Instead, Denmark insisted on defending the Danevirke line in Slesvig and lost everything.

The 1864 defeat led to the continuous build-up of the navy but also to a remarkable and extremely costly expansion of København's defences. To keep it beyond the reach of enemy siege artillery, the capital was enclosed within a huge modern wall system with strong concrete fortresses. Other fortresses were built on the coast and even in the sea. The idea was that Denmark could not hope to win field battles against the German armies but should prepare for a last-ditch defence in 1658-style, hoping for support from France and Britain. There was little hope of Swedish military intervention in the event of a crisis and Norway was ruled by Sweden (until 1905). In fact, Sweden has stayed out of all military conflicts since the Napoleonic Wars.

Denmark, despite its drastically weakened state, still straddled the entrance to the Baltic. Diplomatic efforts were followed by dynastic marriages: one of the daughters of King Christian IX (reign: 1863-1906) was married to a future king of England, another to a future tsar of Russia. One son became king of Greece, another refused to become king of Bulgaria. København's defences were resented by the liberal farmers' party Venstre ('Left'), which opposed the ruling conservative Højre ('Right') party, and became an issue during the period following the new and less progressive democratic constitution of 1866. Only in 1901 was it agreed that the parliamentary majority should form the government (still nominally appointed by the king). In 1915, women were given the right to vote (in 1908 for local elections) – all too late.

The 1866 constitution gave more political influence to the landed gentry. This class owned only 11% of Denmark's agricultural resources (as compared to 78% belonging to farmers and another 11% to small-holders) (see Table 10 on p. 155). The gentry was responsible for most grain exports in what was still a lightly industrialized country. However, two new factors were becoming very important for Denmark's economic development.

Fig. II.19. Thorvaldsens Museum by G. Bindesbøll, 1839+. Photo: Author.

The first was the establishment of cooperatives in which farmers could join forces to compete with the landed gentry. The other was a mass movement away from the cultivation of grain in favour of animal husbandry in the 1880s, with the advent of scientific methods leading to increased yields, for instance of milk and thus of butter. Butter, eggs and bacon became major export items, in particular to England by way of the new port town of Esbjerg in Jylland. Denmark actually became an importer of grain, from Russia among other places. To compensate for the loss of Slesvig and provide land for new small-holders in a rapidly growing population, large areas of heath in Jylland came under the plough. This agricultural expansion also substantially increased the number of archaeological finds.

After the classicizing Empire style, Danish architecture moved towards a conscious use of historical themes, as exemplified by the University Library of 1861, with templates from medieval Italy and a superb use of materials. The round 'Marble Church' (Frederikskirken) of the 1870s was for a long time the romantic ruin of a huge mid-eighteenth-century church, but as it stands today is the most important piece of architecture of this period, reminiscent of the Italian High Renaissance and even of St Peter's in Rome. The most original building, however, is the colourful Thorvaldsen's Museum of 1839 by M.G. Bindesbøll (1800-56), clearly inspired by Roman models but also recalling ancient Egyptian architecture (Fig. II.19). Clearly, the country was making a statement about its place in European history.

While contemporary music was still Romanticist in character, on a par with architecture, a new naturalism saved the literature. J.P.

Jacobsen (1847-85), a great inspiration to contemporary German and British authors, who learned Danish to read him, was a realist, but employed a symbolist language predicting later developments.

Phase XIII. Industrial Society (1864-1950)

By the third quarter of the nineteenth century railways crisscrossed the country while at sea an increasing number of steamers plied the waters. The first railway was opened between København and Roskilde in 1847. By 1875 all areas of Denmark were linked by railways (and ferries). The navy was already using steam frigates during the First Slesvig War. The merchant navy still relied heavily on smaller sailing ships for local transport until after World War I, but steamers were commonly used for longer distances; the first steamer was the *Caledonia* of 1819 serving the important København-Kiel (in Holstein) route linking the capital with the continent. The road system was also considerably improved with paved highways.

Even before World War I Denmark was producing high quality industrial products, steamers, train engines and carriages, factory engines, even early cars and one of the very first planes. Its inventor, J.C.H.-Ellehammer (1871-1946) actually thought he was the first in the world to fly in 1906, unfortunately a couple of years after the Wright Brothers; however, his monoplane was a better design (Fig. II.20). In 1912 Ellehammer flew an originally designed helicopter, five years after a French pioneer. Robust Danish cars were manufactured (the last in 1957), as well as motorcycles (until 1959) and subsequently planes (the last in 1951), alongside high quality weapons for the army. Ships are

Fig. II.20. J.C.H.-Ellehammer in the air, 1906. After Olsen 1988-: vol. 12.

still produced in Denmark in large numbers, including huge container ships and modern warships.

Other products are perhaps better known, like beer from the Carlsberg Breweries established in 1847 by J.C. Jacobsen (1811-87). This company is remarkable for the fact that it donates all its profits to science and the arts. Current production is 750,000 bottles per hour. Carl Jacobsen (1842-1914), J.C. Jacobsen's son, founded the Ny Carlsberg Glyptotek, again using money from beer: a truly remarkable collection of antique and recent European art works, giving København a status equal to European capitals of London, Paris and Berlin in this respect.

Abroad, the Danish Great Nordic telegraph company began to build a line through Russia in 1869 and soon after expanded through China to Japan. Western Europe was incorporated into the network and in 1897 work started on a line via Scotland, the Faroe Islands and Iceland to Greenland and thence to the USA. The company was established by a great industrialist, C.F. Tietgen (1829-1901), also the founder of a surprising number of other major companies of various types. The world's largest shipping company, Mærsk Lines, was founded in Denmark in 1904. (The 400-metre-long M/S *Emma Mærsk* of 2006 is the world's largest container ship.) Denmark was also the first nation to introduce a ship with diesel engines, the deliberately funnel-less *Selandia* of 1912.

In the late nineteenth century massive numbers of people migrated from the countryside to take advantage of better opportunities in the towns, despite the establishment of 100,000 new but fairly small farms. However, life in the towns was not easy and usually short-term was preferred to longer-term migration. Nevertheless, a huge migration to America was taking place (10% of the entire population, in particular many families from German-occupied Slesvig). The creator of photo-journalism in the USA (J. Riis) and the architect of Mount Rushmore – the giant presidents' faces – (G. Børglum) were Danes. At the same time, a substantial Swedish migration to Denmark was taking place, on average a couple of thousand people each year – Denmark, and a less expensive journey, being preferred to the USA. Many Swedes took up employment in rural areas; Polish women arrived to do the same.

Politically, the rise of industrialism and the formation of large groups of town and country workers fuelled socialist movements from 1871 onwards. A Social Democratic party – the future party of the labour unions – was established in 1876 but remained relatively unimportant until after World War I. In outlook the Danes were still farmers, even after leaving the countryside. Almost all industries were small-scale, more similar to craft workshops than to the huge factories of England or Germany. Only rarely did they have more than 100 employees. Life in the towns was not easy for immigrants, but modern hygiene conditions, including clean drinking water and access to medicine and health care, improved conditions, albeit too slowly (see Table 11 on p. 156). Education, always a strong element in Denmark, also helped. A new initiative was adult education at so-called *Højskoler* (literally 'high schools'), particularly widespread in rural areas and aimed at improving the educational level of farmers, old and new.

Højskoler have an almost mythical status in Denmark, almost on a par with Christianity and the welfare state, although their role was already diminishing by the late twentieth century. They represent a liberal, national, Christian ideology, paired with the idea of development through education and knowledge (of the right kind), and are often mentioned in connection with the priest N.F.S. Grundtvig (1783-1872), a powerful poet who supported the movement.

Democratic Denmark was a neutral though heavily armed nation during World War I. As in the Napoleonic Wars a century earlier, it benefited from participation in international trade. Agricultural produce was exported to the states actively engaged in the war, in particular England, Germany and Russia. Between the two World Wars, Denmark's military forces were heavily reduced despite the continuation of the policy of neutrality, with the country being dependent exclusively on its own resources and abilities. In 1917 Denmark's last tropical possessions, the Virgin Islands, were sold to the USA.

After the defeat of Germany in World War I, a referendum in 1920 established the current land border in Slesvig just north of Flensborg town, which had by then gained a German majority: many Germans migrated to the towns of Slesvig after 1864, while many Danes left Slesvig for Denmark or the USA. The Danes in Slesvig suffered heavy discrimination after the Second Slesvig War, with the Danish language being effectively forbidden, reminiscent of the fact that it was an offence in the Skåne provinces won by Sweden to own a book in Danish right up to the mid-nineteenth century. Thousands of Danes in Slesvig served in the German Army during World War I to maintain their properties and to keep at least a part of Slesvig Danish in terms of population. There is still a substantial Danish minority in South Slesvig. After World War II, Danish – and other Scandinavian – social structures, institutions and culture were admired in democratic Germany; the Danish language is widely understood and even spoken in northern Germany.

After the close of World War II, Denmark turned down an Allied proposal to move the border southwards. The rationale behind this decision was to keep the country as homogeneous as possible in terms of population, culture and language. Ironically, recent immigration, in particular of Muslims, has created problems far greater than those of a smaller German minority in Slesvig. At any rate, joint Danish-German membership of NATO and of the European Union after World War II has made these considerations obsolete.

By the turn of the century, the power of the right-wing party in the parliament was finally broken and a left-wing (liberal) government formed. Denmark's political fabric was also changing, not least because the new small farmers and workers were beginning to acquire a political voice. A splinter liberal party (the radical left) and in particular the social democrats (labour) conditioned the political stage, not least in the wake of the world economic crises of the 1920s and 1930s. The social democratic party was the main creator of the welfare state, to which most Danes still subscribe. A welfare state is like a farmers' village: mutual support but also limitations.

Only a few Danes flirted with the dictatorships of the 1930s, made unreceptive by, among other things, anti-German sentiments, tolerance and humour. One sympathizer was Niels E.M. Bukh (1880-1950), a gymnastics teacher and headmaster of a fine *højskole* for athletes, who toured the world with his disciplined and well-trained amateur teams; he made a lasting impact on Communist Russia (USSR), Imperial Japan and certainly Nazi Germany, worshipping a new healthy race of soldiers, workers and wives. In sports, the Danes are among the best in the world at sailing, cycling and, sometimes, ball sports. Amateur sentiments still run high, despite the prevalent commercial professionalism.

T. Stauning (1873-1942) was Denmark's first Social Democratic minister and Prime Minister (1924-26; 1929-42). The 1930s were crisis years with very high unemployment and difficulties for agriculture, highly dependent on export. Nevertheless, Danish society was stable. A social reform bill was passed in 1933 and in the 1935 election the Social Democrats obtained 46% of the vote. The idea of a territorial defence of Denmark was virtually abolished, in spite of Hitler's ascent to power in Germany in 1933. The government's position was that Germany could overwhelm Denmark whenever it wished; there were also concerns about a German occupation of the parts of Slesvig won by referendum after World War I. Instead, the social fabric was strengthened in the face of totalitarian ideologies. The acceptance of the German occupation in 1940, virtually without combat, was a consequence of this policy: national survival was the number one priority.[1]

The atmosphere in Denmark before World War II was optimistic and modernist, as demonstrated by the architecture of a major provincial town like Ålborg in North Jylland, where a new airport and a new bridge across the Limfjord were linked to a new boulevard lined with elegant

---

[1] A combative Denmark, mining the Belts and defending crucial harbours and airports for a while, would have suffered gravely. But this action might have saved Norway from German occupation (a risky gamble that cost Germany dearly in lost warships), since the Royal Navy was on the verge of occupying Norwegian harbours. The outcome would have been to alter the course of World War II, denying Germany direct access to the North Atlantic, including the Allied supply routes to the USSR from 1941 onwards.

buildings (Jensen 2003). Even the commercial production of planes was started. The main architect of this novelty in Ålborg was the son-in-law of the Social Democratic mayor, who even arranged for a council meeting to take place in the air. An exhibition held in 1933 was a milestone: the fine steel tower on a hill (with a restaurant at the top) is still one of Ålborg's main attractions. In line with Social Democratic ambitions, old neighbourhoods were demolished to provide modern housing with toilets inside each apartment, as well as hot and cold running water and a bath, a kitchen stove, central heating, electricity and so forth – for everyone (cf. Table 11 on p. 156). Both Prime Minister Stauning and members of the royal family were present on various official occasions.

On the day of the German occupation, 9 April 1940, the new airport at Ålborg was captured by 1400 German parachute troops, the first such operation in military history. Control of the airport was an important factor in the simultaneous occupation of Norway, where fighting continued in the mountains until the summer. During World War II, Sweden remained neutral: initially leaning more towards Germany, selling high-quality iron ore to Germany and allowing German troops to pass through Swedish territory into Norway, and more towards the Allies by the end. Concerns about Finland, supported by Germany in its struggle against Communist Russia (Communism never gained a firm foothold in Scandinavia), were an important issue.

Denmark embarked on a policy of self-government in collaboration with Germany. A free election was even held in March 1943 (giving the Nazi Party less than 2% of the vote) (see Table 12 on p. 156). Denmark's goal – officially and unofficially – was to safeguard the country and prevent a change in its status under occupation; a policy supported by Sweden. However, the government was forced to resign in the summer of 1943, leaving its administration in the hands of the heads of the ministerial offices (much as in the days of the absolute monarchy); decrees were acknowledged by the high court and the king remained in the country. On the same day that the government resigned, the Danish armed forces managed to sink most of the fairly strong navy before being arrested (the Air Force was destroyed on the ground in 1940). In October 1943 nearly all of Denmark's several thousand Jews were smuggled across to neutral and unoccupied Sweden by the resistance (with tacit help from the German Army). The Danish police were arrested in 1944 and sent to concentration camps in Germany.

The incipient resistance movement was an important card in the hands of the Danish government and civil service, since Germany did not wish to have an openly rebellious Denmark at its rear. Resistance started on a larger scale in 1942 but was suppressed as long as the Danish government remained in place. An underground government, 'The Council of Freedom', was established when the actual government resigned; in 1944 this body was acknowledged by the Allies. Sabotage increased as British weapons and explosives were air-dropped to the resistance movement. Militarily, the most important actions were sabotage of the railways in Jylland, delaying German troops on their way from Norway and Denmark (see Fig. III.33). The German occupation ended on 5 May 1945.

Optimism and energy were characteristic of the sciences in the early nineteenth century. Professional institutions were founded, channelling outstanding individual achievements into concrete results and the education of the younger generations. Danish Nobel Prize winners in the sciences include N.R. Finsen (1860-1904) for medicine in 1903 for his treatment of skin tuberculosis using light; he also realized the power of chemically active ultraviolet light in fighting and preventing other diseases. S. August S. Krogh (1874-1949) received the Nobel Prize for physiology in 1920 for the so-called capillary motor regulating system, demonstrating that the absorption of oxygen and elimination of carbon dioxide in the lungs take place by diffusion and not by regulation on the part of the organism. During a stay in USA in 1922 Krogh leaned about insulin (used to treat diabetes) and obtained a licence to purify it. Upon his return, he founded what is now one of the world's largest pharmaceutical companies, Novo Nordisk.

Niels H.D. Bohr (1885-1962) received the Nobel Prize for physics in 1922 for research based on the earlier discovery of the atomic nucleus. By introducing concepts borrowed from quantum theory, Bohr succeeded in developing a picture of the atomic structure. His later work contributed to the knowledge leading to the nuclear bomb. Bohr developed the concept of complementarity which challenged Newton's system of physics; he even took an interest in molecular biology, an immensely important scientific field today. During the German occupation of Denmark, Bohr was smuggled out of the country to prevent his knowledge being used by the Germans (nuclear fission was discovered in Germany in 1938). A son of Niels Bohr also received the Nobel Prize (1975).

Danes have also won Nobel Prizes for medicine, chemistry (1997, the most recent), peace and literature, including Johannes V. Jensen (1873-1950) in 1944. Cinema and music are not considered by the Nobel Prize committee (nor are the humanities or social sciences). The Danish cinema of the early twentieth century – a distant forerunner of the current wave – deserved this type of recognition, with C.T. Dreyer (1889-1968) being world-renowned for his understated style. Denmark's great national composer of this period is Carl Nielsen (1865-1931), popularizing what is perceived as a Danish sound.

As always, architecture is a reflection of society. The close of the nineteenth century sees a continuation of the search for historical models but put together in novel and self-conscious ways. Observing that such architecture is commonplace in Europe, the psychological

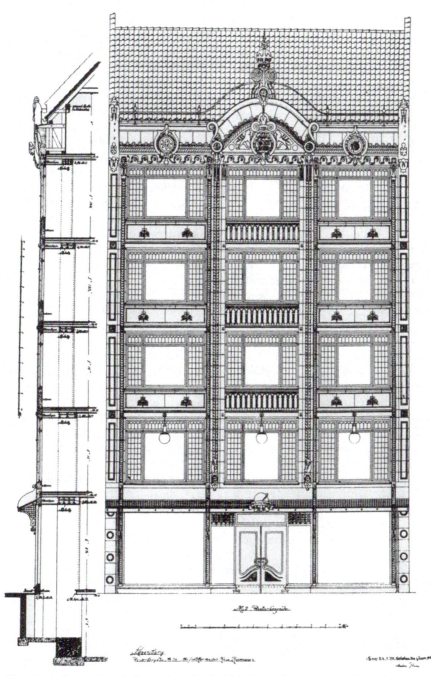

Fig. II.21. Savoy Hotel ('Løvenborg') of 1906: Vesterbrogade 34, København.
Architect A. Rosen. After From and Jensen 2003.

explanation is likely a positive response to change, with history – in Denmark often local history – providing a sense of stability. An example is the Ny Carlsberg Glyptotek in København (1890) with its interesting interior, including a palm garden. An appealing structure is the lavish Jesuskirken (Jesus Church), København (1885). A. Rosen (1859-1928) is highly personal and detailed in his architectural style, inspired by the continental Jugend Style. The Jugend emerged as a reaction against Historicism, but was nevertheless historical in reference and ambition. Rosen's Savoy Hotel (or 'Løvenborg') in København (1906) is a true gem (with modern load-bearing elements in steel allowing for very large windows) (Fig. II.21). His elegant Palace Hotel, København (1906+/1910) strives to define bourgeois elitism as a token of economic progress and inventive solidity. This world, seriously shaken by World War I, also produced a marvellous designer: Georg Jensen (1866-1935), known especially for his acclaimed silverware, still produced and sold internationally. The rich and inventive architecture and crafts of the period before World War I are still not fully appreciated, clouded as they are in the mist of Modernist critique.

Painters and sculptors were legion during this phase. Vilhelm Hammershøi (1864-1916) should perhaps be singled out for his restrained yet vibrant motifs showing city interiors in grey tones; he, too, is represented at the National Gallery in London. Very different is another internationally well-known figure, P.S. Krøyer (1851-1909), with his virtuoso paintings of sympathetic people in the summer light. Visiting European art museums, it is striking how much the painting of this period varies from country to country: a characteristic Danish 'programme' is also identifiable, as in literature, music, architecture, the applied arts, crafts and so on – indeed, in everything aesthetic and material.

Among Denmark's writers, it is worth mentioning Karen C. Blixen (1885-1962, English pseudonyms Isak Dinesen and Pierre Andrezel). Her at once complex and simple, and rather aloof style, often taken for typically 'Danish' by foreigners, is deliberately archaic and international. The literature of this phase is very rich indeed, leading to three Nobel Prizes, but is relatively little known abroad due to the obstacle of the Danish language. Poetry in particular, highly suited to the flexible Danish tongue, is virtually impossible to translate. Henrik Pontoppidan (1857-1943; Nobel Prize winner in 1917) is known for his moving realism. A short story on the life and death of a very poor family's one fattening pig recounts the father's bitter and desperate thoughts: that it would have been better had one of the children died.

One building standing outside the currents of time is the huge brick Grundtvig's Church in København of 1913 (built 1921-27) by P.V. Jensen-Klindt (1853-1930). Evidently inspired by medieval Late Gothic architecture, and thus Historicist, it is nevertheless Modernist in its insistence on simplified and transformed parts as the new whole. We might even see a reactionary 'Post-Modernist' discourse in this simultaneously remarkable and confusing structure surrounded by a contemporary apartment block development.

A reaction against complexity took place after World War I with simple Modernist (Functionalist) architecture such as Arne Jacobsen's (1902-71) apartment building at Bellevue, right on the Øresund to the north of København (1934), his masterly petrol station nearby (1936), the Århus town hall (1942), and, among his later buildings, St Catherine's College, University of Oxford (1964). Reinforced concrete (rather than the traditional brick) was now coming into use (in as early as 1908). Internationally, Jacobsen is perhaps best known for his 'Danish' geometrical-organic chairs and other indoor items. Indeed, the handcrafted Danish furniture of this phase, designed by many different fine architects and today too costly to produce, is much appreciated: small and elegant artworks for the home. The critical architect Poul Henningsen (1894-1967) is famous for his lamps giving indirect light (almost every other Danish home has one), lighting being an essential part of Danish well-being at home: things never forgotten when living in the country – interior design, light fixtures arranged in particular ways, even small items experienced as 'Danish'. The human mind has a peculiar and almost archaeological talent for reading objects, buildings, settlements, landscapes (and other human beings): the basis for emotional attachment.

Phase XIV. Modernization (1950-2000)

After World War II, Denmark changed from being a predominantly agricultural society to a country dominated by towns and industrial production – paying for social welfare, including free education at all levels, free health care, support for the elderly, unemployment benefits and pensions, public libraries, sporting facilities and so forth. Today, a high-yield agricultural sector geared for export is run by a mere few percent of the population with the help of robots to feed and milk the cows and clean the barns. In the countryside, buildings reminiscent of 'old times' are transformed into week-end homes, parts of suburbia or new 'towns' along motorways where transport companies, warehouses and some manufacturing industries cluster, thus transforming century-old settlement patterns. Suburban society expanded dramatically with the new-found wealth of the 1950s; whole neighbourhoods sprang up in egalitarian style with identical-sized homes, and most households soon had a car of their own. High-rise buildings also became popular, a symbol of modernity and progress, but have now largely been abandoned as an architectural idiom: isolating families and giving rise to crime. A symbol of the early welfare state is the beautiful Bellahøj housing estate of the 1940s; unknown to most, it stands on the site of the Swedish

Fig. II.22. Bellahøj housing estate 1944/1950+. Architects Mogens Irming & Tage Nielsen; Svenn Eske Kristensen, Edvard Heiberg, Karl Larsen, Ole Buhl, Harald Petersen, Dan Fink; C. Th. Sørensen. Photo: Author.

Karlstad fortress from the siege of København 1658-60 (Fig. II.22; cf. Fig. III.24).

The Social Democrats, like other political parties, strongly supported a capitalist economy, providing the income necessary to fund social welfare. The costs of the welfare state increased dramatically and have now begun to undermine the concept itself: not everyone can be on the receiving end. It was above all the services sector that changed Danish society, and now another transformation is taking place, turning Denmark into a country where goods are taken for granted; services remain important but the speed of information has become a crucial issue. The entry of women into the workforce, in particular from the 1960s onwards, has been very important; today nearly all Danish women work outside the home.

Economic expansion in Denmark gave the state access to unprecedented wealth in the form of taxes and duties (VAT is 25%). For a time there seemed to be no end to progress, but when taxes reached the 50% mark and unemployment, for instance, became a benefit rather than a burden, the welfare state could expand no longer. Its values remain, however, and both old and new activities require funding, something possible only through cuts and higher productivity. Behind the growth of a modern society lie both an active public sector and a flexible private one.

Sweden, which stayed out of both World Wars, spearheaded post-World War II development in Scandinavia and in many ways served as a model for Denmark. The difference between the two countries is that Social Democrats and Socialists have rarely formed a majority in the Danish parliament, while the opposite has been the case in Sweden until recently, with the Swedish Social Democrats virtually 'owning' the country. Social welfare policies brought Sweden to virtual bankruptcy in the early 1990s, with its currency dropping 40% in value (it is even weaker today). Only the fall of the Berlin Wall in 1989, allowing for a very significant reduction in Swedish military spending, saved the country from further economic decline. We should add that the strong social fabric of a welfare state proved its worth, even though Sweden is still recovering. There is also a strong tradition in Sweden, stemming from the days of the militarized seventeenth and eighteenth centuries, of holding leaders in high respect and avoiding open discussion. Letters from readers, for instance, are unknown in Swedish newspapers.

Economic growth gained impetus in the late 1950s, supported by a global economic expansion led by the USA. The independence of the colonies in the developing world also provided grounds for optimism, however difficult the situation may be today. The Communist leader J.V. Stalin died (1953) and optimism pervaded the world, despite the suppressed Hungarian uprising (1956) and the Cuban crisis of 1962 that almost led to nuclear war between East and West. The USSR opened up slightly, but it took until the late 1980s – and the courage of First Secretary M. Gorbachev – to alter the fabric of the Communist superpower and allow for the fall of the Berlin Wall (1989), built in 1961 to safeguard Communist East Germany (DDR).

Denmark has been a member of the United Nations (UN) and of the North Atlantic Treaty Organization (NATO) since their foundation (1945 and 1949 respectively). To become a member of an international defence alliance was a great step for a country hitherto without treaty allies, but one made necessary by international circumstances, in particular the threat from Communist Russia and its allies in occupied eastern Europe (Norway is also a member of NATO, but Sweden and Finland are not). Attempts to create a Nordic defence alliance were not successful, nor was economic integration. Despite their cultural and other similarities, the economic structures of the Nordic countries differ significantly.

Denmark became a member of the European Union (EU) in 1972. In this context an important issue is diminishing sovereignty as the EU moves from being merely an economic body ensuring free trade to an organization which attempts to regulate society and even culture. Cross-border movement between member states is now completely free and a common currency (the Euro) has been introduced, albeit not yet in Denmark. Norway, whose oil resources make it a very wealthy country, is not a member of the EU. Nor are the North Atlantic nations, due particularly to their fear of losing exclusive fishing and other rights over their offshore territories. Denmark is self-sufficient in oil (from the North Sea); wind-power accounts for more than 20% of its energy.

An interesting side-effect of post-World War II wealth and education was the development of a youth culture, sometimes a rebellious one, as in 1968. In Denmark, such movements often mimic those abroad but are nevertheless the outcome of a quest by the post-war generations to develop new qualities and aspirations in all walks of life, including freedom of expression, engagement, personal life, consumption and travel. These movements gave rise to soulful Danish rock music, in part replacing the jazz of previous generations. A special phenomenon is the 40-year-old 'Free City' of Christiania in the centre of København, a self-organized community and bastion of individualism. Cheap charter flights turned Europe and later the world into a personal experience for almost everyone from the 1960s onwards. Access to international TV channels has proved less important given their heavily commercial nature.

The old values of industrial societies and the struggle for social equality waned in the face of these developments. New groups of people, typically from the unruly Balkans and the Near East, were admitted into Denmark. Immigration was vital for economic expansion, in particular in the services sector, but it also posed cultural challenges. The socially and culturally homogeneous Denmark which emerged after the Slesvig Wars and as a result of its long democratic development, now had to deal with the world's problems on its own doorstep. The decline of traditional values and the arrival of large groups of Muslims – difficult to integrate and often poorly educated even in the second and third generations – necessitate a new political agenda for Denmark. By contrast, the recent arrival of large numbers of East Europeans has posed relatively few problems.

In this environment, we should be particularly wary of the economic recession which in some countries, including the USA and Iceland, has been extremely serious and will no doubt have an impact on Denmark, highly dependent as it is on exports. However, as of the summer of 2009, the country has suffered only slightly from these international economic difficulties. Cautious Denmark, which has possibly the world's strongest economy, a strong social fabric and a strong currency, is well prepared for financial crises and depression (see Table 13 on p. 157).

Denmark's secret weapon remains the highly educated employees of fairly small and highly flexible companies integrated in a well-tuned economy dependent on exports. Interestingly, company-based education is on the rise, while the general training offered by traditional public

Fig. II.23. Grande Arche de la Défense of 1983, Paris. Architect J.O. von Spreckelsen (1929-87).

institutions such as universities is becoming less important. Technological inventions have compensated for the loss of traditional industries such as textiles, furniture, kitchen utensils, printing, radios and so forth, although Bang & Olufsen high-quality radios and TV-sets are world renowned, not least for their superb design, and Lego toys are still very popular. The medical industry is another case in point – *Antabus*, a Danish medicine for alcoholism, recently celebrated its sixtieth anniversary. Danish windmills and aquatic products are world leading, as are the Danish measuring instruments used on space missions.

J. Utzon (1918-2008) is possibly the best-known architect of this phase in Danish history with his 60-metre-high multiple shell-shaped Sydney Opera House (1956) exploiting the potential of concrete to the utmost. Henning Larsen (1925-) is known for his Foreign Office in Riyadh, Saudi Arabia, of 1982, a playful modernist structure for a future Islam. The impressive square white-marble Grande Arche de la Défense in Paris of 1983 is by J.O. von Spreckelsen (1929-87) (Fig. II.23). The evocative oblique Black Diamond – the Royal Library extension on the København waterfront, clad in pure black marble – was built in 1999 (by the firm of Schmidt, Hammer & Lassen) and gave København an architectural monument ranking with the aforementioned works built by Danes in foreign countries. Clearly, attempts to turn buildings into psychological templates or art are characteristic of this age. Many foreign artists worked in Denmark in the eighteenth century and earlier, but only recently have foreign architects once again been active in the country; they include D. Libeskind (1946-) with his artful Danish Jewish Museum, N. Foster (1935-) with a fine new Elephant House for København Zoo, and J. Nouvel (1945-) with a dream-like concert hall: a semi-transparent blue cube from the outside, the interior in wooden scales.

But highlights are one thing. For ordinary homes and offices the economic benefits of a simple industrial Functionalist style were evident until it ran out of steam and added post-Modernist historical references to the same slightly inhuman structures. Today's building boom is unprecedented, but the difficulty of combining low price, beauty and a contemporary feel remains. The sublime structures mentioned above have no such problems. The architecture of many countries strives for greatness, Danish architecture for simplicity and modesty, a national shyness perhaps.

Very different in nature are the 'wild' paintings and decorative abstractions of the so-called COBRA movement – an acronym of København, Brussels, Amsterdam – of around 1950, virtually in opposition to contemporary architecture. Among the many artists of this phase Per Kierkeby (1938-), educated as a geologist, should perhaps be singled out for his perception of objects and his multifaceted talent. More original is I. Cronhammer (1947-); his gigantic iron plate landscape sculpture 'Elia' at Herning, in the shape of a cupola with four staircases leading to four columns, is a major work of Danish art (see p. 113). The beautiful 'Louisiana' art museum of 1958, situated right on the Øresund, summarizes much of Denmark's artistic life after World War II.

Literature is again little known outside Denmark. Poet Inger Christensen (1935-2009) has created symbolist interpretations of modern life. Peter Høeg (1957-) has attracted international attention for his free rein novels. In cinema, the 'Dogma School' headed by Lars von Trier (1956-) is much acclaimed and also influential abroad. The director Susanne Bier (1960-) addresses everyday themes in colourful and imaginative ways. Per Nørgård (1932-) is probably the most prominent contemporary composer, his music bordering on chaos; *At the End of the Day* is the characteristic title of his sixth symphony (2000). Cultural life is truly booming, almost as in the golden days of the early nineteenth century, but now supported by a strong economy.

Towards the end of the twentieth century, computers were becoming a normal possession, the great step being the affordable PCs of the 1980s. TV was commonplace by a quarter of a century earlier, as was broadcast radio in the period between the two World Wars. Long holidays and a shorter working week provided ample time for travel and

Fig. II.24. Store Bælt Bridge, which opened in the late 1990s.

a great many leisure and educational activities, enjoyed by all irrespective of income. Denmark is in every way one of the most egalitarian societies in the world, not least due to the very high level of education. Communication has been greatly improved with new motorways and not least two major bridges (with dams and tunnels), the longest across open waters in the world: over the Store Bælt (opened in the late 1990s) (Fig. II.24) and across the Øresund to old Skåne (opened in 2000).

Denmark, practically turning its back on its maritime past, thus became a compact and integrated unit with concomitant strengths and relatively few weaknesses. This transformation occurred during a period of renewed expansion: an economy seeing very high employment and drawing in workers from neighbouring countries, including Sweden and Germany, as well the new eastern Europe. The airport at København is the largest in northern Europe.

Phase XV. Globalization

Fifteen millennia after the arrival of *Homo Sapiens* hunters on the territory that was to become Denmark, Europe and the world challenged the country far beyond mere contact and traditional trade relations.

In April 1994, seven Danish tanks and an armoured car relieved a UN post in Bosnia. The Danish troops came under heavy fire en route. They

Fig. II.25. *Absalon* naval support ship, 2004.

decided to return fire, destroying Serbian bunkers and other positions, and an ammunitions dump; the outcome was several hundred enemy casualties (there were no Danish losses). The skirmish put an end to the Serbian genocide of Muslims and the humiliation of UN peace-keeping forces. For Denmark, the 'The battle at Tuzla' meant that the country, not having engaged larger enemy forces since 1940 (or more accurately 1864), accepted a fighting peace-keeping role abroad, including in Iraq and Afghanistan.

This role is supported by a fairly large air force dominated by fighter planes, armoured battalions and two large heavily armed flexible 7,000 tonne 'support ships' whose armaments include missiles, torpedoes and guns firing GPS-guided shells distances of over 100 km (Fig. II.25). These vessels, the largest ever in the Danish navy, each have the ability to land 200 special troops and more than 50 vehicles, and to serve in other capacities (command platform, mine-layer, emergency ship, hospital); the ships also carry large helicopters and landing craft. The first armed patrol was used as the headquarters for the international force launched against pirates off the Horn of Africa. Three similar 'patrol vessels' (the Danish euphemism for heavy missile frigates) will be assigned active roles, supported by smaller modern vessels. Significantly, the first of the new ships are named after Archbishop Absalon of the Middle Ages (died 1201) and his brother (see above, p. 47f.). Submarines – highly suited to the Baltic and Denmark's coastal waters – have been scrapped, perhaps a mistake.

The warships are symbols of Denmark's global engagement under the aegis of its alliances, securing political good-will and providing guarantees. The same is true of the massive aid given to developing countries and international organizations, administered by DANIDA/Danish Foreign Office; the highest in the world in terms of GNP (and other factors).

Denmark is not immune to outside influence and is often drawn directly into the world's problems, both at home and abroad. With the country taking on an active role in land-locked Afghanistan, these problems are becoming increasingly complex. Denmark's economy is heavily dependent on international trade and transportation. It is also vulnerable to changes in the world financial market – increasingly centred on London – and to the implications of the movement and investment of capital. For instance, Saudi Arabian investments are usually accompanied by demands which the western world considers undemocratic or even dangerous. A rather more insidious problem is pollution, which obviously crosses political borders. The much-discussed climate change also has global ramifications.

A couple of decades ago, fears of another Ice Age dominated and a glacial episode will no doubt occur. However, a research team from the Danish Space Centre headed by H. Svensmark (1958-) has resuscitated a theory regarding the influence on the climate of cosmic radiation from exploding stars. The group has convincingly demonstrated that there is a strong positive correlation over millions of years between cosmic radiation and low cloud cover: low clouds imply a cooling of the atmosphere (Svensmark et al. 2007; Svensmark 2007). Cosmic radiation has dropped by 15% over the past 100 years, explaining the recent rise in average temperature of 0.7°. The political fall-out from the findings of the Danish team is still awaited as the international 'CO$_2$ lobby' is very strong, tending to blame humanity for all misery, perhaps in the political hope that humanity should be able to remedy all problems.

Nonetheless, Denmark is located in a favourable geographical, cultural and social niche in Europe and the world, shaped by its long history, specific experiences and attitudes, and therefore also particular interests and responsibilities.

The sharply expanding internet is the most dramatic recent change in the life of nearly everyone, rivalled only by the mobile phone: the world at your own desk, or at your ear and fingertips if we think of the brilliant

SMS-systems. It is difficult to imagine anything that could change the world, or Denmark, to the same extent in the decades to come. But crucial technological novelties will doubtless emerge all the same, such as optic invisibility, micro-robots and medical cures for cancer and other serious diseases, enabling us to stop seeing the world as only a dangerous place.

Conclusions

Engang du herre var i hele Norden,
bød over England, – nu du kaldes svag ,...

Once lord in all the North,
Bade over England, – now weak you're called, ...
                                        Hans Christian Andersen, 1850

Earlier we summarized the period from the Ice Age to about AD 1200, a time of enormous change but also of expansion. Expansion continued in the thirteenth century with new towns being founded and old ones refounded with special rights. The development of agriculture and settlements are much debated; seemingly, there was a marked population decline in the fourteenth century, hastened by the plague or Black Death. Animal husbandry became more important towards the end of the Middle Ages, including the export of cattle.

The Late Middle Ages saw a marked growth of towns, in particular in the Øresund region, including København. Around (and before) 1500, country churches were modernized in the Gothic style: an immense investment, made at the same time as town churches and monasteries, alongside manor houses and town mansions, also in brick, were being built. These monuments have all become part of a specifically Danish heritage, albeit inspired by mercantile northern Germany, in particular Lübeck.

The Protestant Reformation (1536) not only led to a new distribution of wealth (with the confiscation of church properties) but also embraced the new architectural idiom of the Renaissance, acquired from further south and west in Europe. The Renaissance is manifest in many castles and manor houses in Denmark: another highly valued heritage, for its tourism potential among other things.

Wars with Sweden, a result of the crumbling Nordic Union of 1397, characterize the middle centuries of the first millennium AD, culminating in the seventeenth century with the loss of East Denmark (except Bornholm), one fifth of its parishes and probably more in terms of population; certainly more in terms of total resources.

Nevertheless, Denmark recovered as a great merchant nation,

111

reorganizing its agricultural system and saving its forests. Unfortunately, the Napoleonic Wars brought conflict with Great Britain over precisely such mercantile affairs, the navy was ceded and Denmark's union with Norway terminated (Norway won independence from Sweden only in 1905).

A remarkable artistic and scientific golden age followed, releasing bourgeois energies in a nation-state freed of imperial responsibilities. The rise of democratic Denmark was marred by a nationalistic conflict and even by two wars with the German nation over Slesvig-Holstein, ending with Bismarck's conquest of the whole region. Yet Denmark once again recovered, hesitantly entering the industrial age, promoting education and agricultural expansion, and accepting all challenges.

The country stayed out of World War I but not World War II, when it was occupied by Nazi Germany. The Occupation was a balance between reluctant collaboration on everyday matters and an increasingly open resistance. After the war came collaboration with the western powers and – for the first time – membership of a military alliance: NATO. A remarkable increase in wealth promoted the welfare state, already founded in the 1930s. This system grew with rising production but suffered from taxation rates above 50%, alongside VAT of 25%.

Current global challenges are adding to these difficulties, as is the immigration of mainly unskilled people from very different cultural backgrounds. Nevertheless, Denmark has a highly talented and well-educated population and certainly one of the strongest economies in the world, not least because it has its own sources of energy. The country is superbly managed, natural areas with old towns mixing with economic landscapes and an impressive capital (Cook 2006).

Denmark's archaeological past and history are both long and extremely rich. Doubtless the country has survived the threat of annihilation thanks to the respect it inspired in other nations, its strong social and cultural fabric, and a particular protection – the Danish language. Today Denmark's gross national product is very high indeed and there seems to be no end to its prosperity. The reason for this is an extremely active public sector (including education) and a very successful and flexible private sector. But democracy is by far its greatest asset.

No doubt Denmark's neutral status during World War I and its intelligent survival strategy during World War II were beneficial to recent development, even though a recent Prime Minister (now secretary general of NATO) has declared non-military resistance an act of cowardice: probably a reminder to countries and pressure groups using techniques reminiscent of the totalitarian regimes of Europe in the 1930s. The strongest pressure group of all remains the political and administrative system.

North Sea oil is a special asset, as is wind power, which meets more than 20% of the country's energy needs. The friendly relationship with

Greenland will also ensure availability of the northern world's resources in the future. The loss of almost all of East Denmark to Sweden in 1658 is the single greatest tragedy experienced by the country during its history, but has been compensated for by Nordic and EU integration, and by the Øresund Bridge. The loss of southern Slesvig is deplorable (the status of Flensborg town – the second largest in the country – might even have been resolved to the benefit of Denmark).

Finally, a question: why has little Denmark – the world's oldest kingdom – been so successful on the European and even the world stage (see Table 13 on p. 157)? A simple answer: because of the status and accomplishments of the past and the experience thus gained, including a particular talent for cultural selection and social management, engagement and delivery.

Fig. II.26. Iron plate sculpture 'Elia' at Herning, Jylland, by I. Cronhammer (2000). It is 60 metres in diameter and 11 metres high at the platform (total height 30 metres); the columns are capped with red lights. On certain days a high flame flares up between the columns. Photo: Author.

Part III

Topics and Tables

Topics

1. Jordehøj Passage Grave

Jordehøj is a superb passage grave of the late fourth millennium BC on the island of Møn (Dehn et al. 2000). Restoration has yielded detailed information on its construction, including drainage ditches with a fill of crushed flint along and between some of the orthostats, as well as packings of flint, chalk and stone. The main aim was to keep the chamber and passage dry. To this end, birch bark was placed between the flat stone slabs in the so-called dry stone walls between the orthostats.

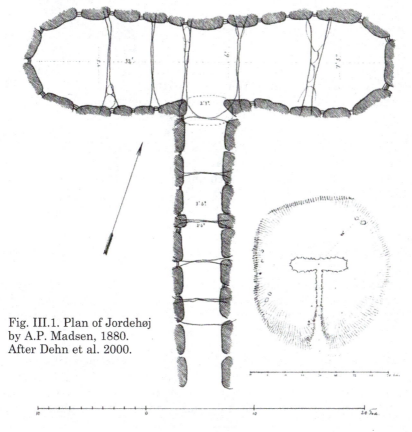

Fig. III.1. Plan of Jordehøj
by A.P. Madsen, 1880.
After Dehn et al. 2000.

117

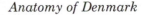

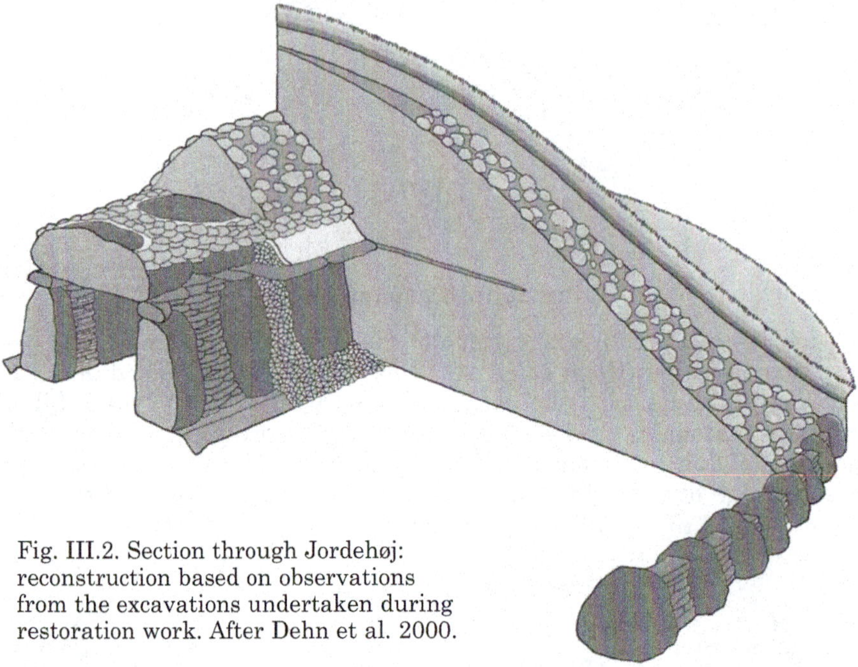

Fig. III.2. Section through Jordehøj:
reconstruction based on observations
from the excavations undertaken during
restoration work. After Dehn et al. 2000.

Some artefacts found in the chamber belong to the Funnel-Beaker
Culture, while others are from Late Neolithic secondary burials,
suggesting a period of ritual use of over 1,000 years. Unfortunately the
previously excavated smaller finds, such as the skeletal remains, are
rather poorly documented, unlike the construction of the monument.
Below Jordehøj, traces of plough-marks were clearly visible.

A nearby double passage-grave at Klekkendehøj presents large steps
in the stone-packing on top of the chamber, all covered by the mound.

2. Kivik Grave

The Kivik ('Ki-cove') grave of *c.* 1300 BC consists of a three-metre-long
stone cist in a huge cairn (75 metres in diameter) on a beach in East Skåne
(Randsborg 1993). The cist is orientated north-south and was uncovered
in 1748. A few years later it was realized that the eight slabs on the long
sides held framed rock-carvings forming part of a picture programme.

Excavations revealed the remains of a bossed bronze cauldron, a
bronze sword (or dagger), a fibula and, perhaps, a double button for the
sword belt. The cauldron has a parallel in a grave on Bornholm
containing the heaviest gold ring found in a grave from the entire Nordic
Bronze Age. Obviously, the Kivik man was a king ('*Ki*'?). Kivik, with a
'nature' suffix, might be among the oldest existing place-names.
Incidentally, *Ki* means 'place' in third-millennium Mesopotamian.

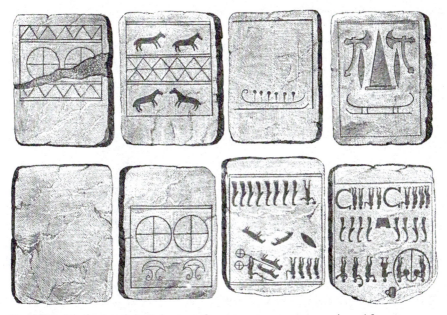

Fig. III.3. Kivik cist slabs: nineteenth-century copper engraving. After Randsborg 1993. The slabs are depicted tilted outwards.

The following pictures can be seen on the slabs (beginning from the south-east, i.e. top right of Fig. III.3): (1) a tall brimmed hat flanked by two cult axes above a model ship. The hat was either feathered or had two swords flanking it – a symbol of the Sun God; (2) Two manned ships; (3) two times two horses (the horses that pull the sun across the sky?); 'two' indicates repetition; (4) two wheel-crosses: symbols of movement and of the sun (cf. the wheels on horse-drawn chariots); (5) obliterated motif; (6) two mushroom-shaped symbols: perhaps symbolizing the movements of the sun, perhaps simply 'night'; (7) at the top, a horse-drawn chariot and a group of warriors (swords); in the middle, a series of 'unruly' wild animals (symbolizing nature?); at the bottom, a procession of sad-looking cowled women (?) led by a dancing man; (8) at the very top, a huge cup-mark and linked to it a ring of equal size (solstice?); below this and on the same level as the chariot etc. on the previous panel, a series of ritual scenes including a possible duel or dance (in a circular framed area), a display of artefacts and the blowing of *lur* trumpets; in the scene below, cowled figures are gathered at the sides of a large item, perhaps a grave and possibly even the Kivik cist; at the bottom there is also a double motif: a procession of men marching towards the opening of a very large *omega*-figure (gateway?).

A structural interpretation of slabs (7) and (8) gives: (7) aristocratic level above nature above underworld; (8) heaven above aristocratic

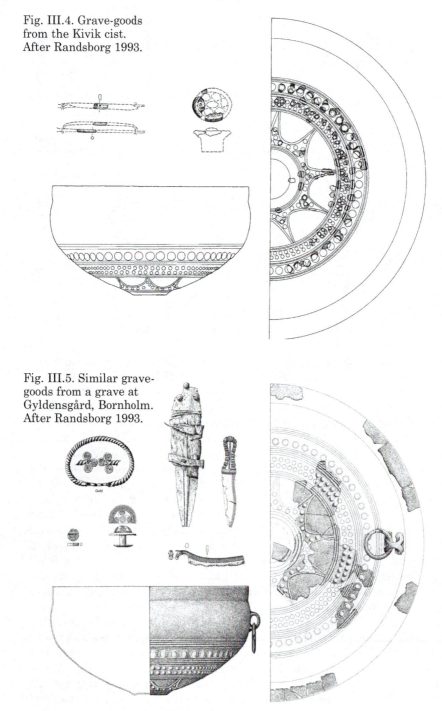

Fig. III.4. Grave-goods
from the Kivik cist.
After Randsborg 1993.

Fig. III.5. Similar grave-
goods from a grave at
Gyldensgård, Bornholm.
After Randsborg 1993.

world above underworld meeting the living (upon burial?) above underworld. An interpretation of the scenes as one long procession is less likely.

3. Bronze Age Cosmology

Bronze Age cosmology is based on the worship and study of the sun. The famous Early Bronze Age model sun-chariot of the fourteenth century BC from Trundholm Bog on Sjælland shows the sun driving its horse across the skies (Randsborg and Christensen 2006). The golden side of the decorated disc is turned towards the observer when the sun moves from left to right, east to west; the dark side without gold is turned towards the observer (and the earth) when the sun – not shining – moves from right to left, back to sunrise. The model stands on a wagon with four-spoked chariot wheels, symbols of speed and even of the moving sun itself.

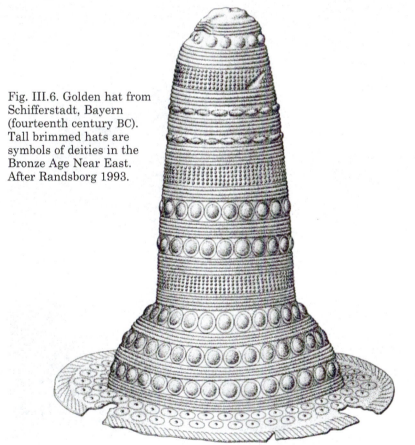

Fig. III.6. Golden hat from Schifferstadt, Bayern (fourteenth century BC). Tall brimmed hats are symbols of deities in the Bronze Age Near East. After Randsborg 1993.

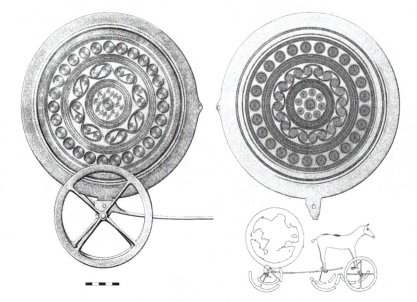

Fig. III.7. Sun-
chariot from
Trundholm Bog,
Sjælland. Early
Bronze Age, four-
teenth century BC.
After Randsborg
and Christensen
2006.

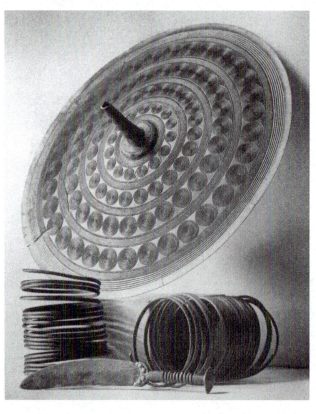

Fig. III.8. Belt-plate
from Langstrup Bog,
Sjælland, with other
items from the find.
Bronze Age, four-
teenth century BC.
After Randsborg and
Christensen 2006.

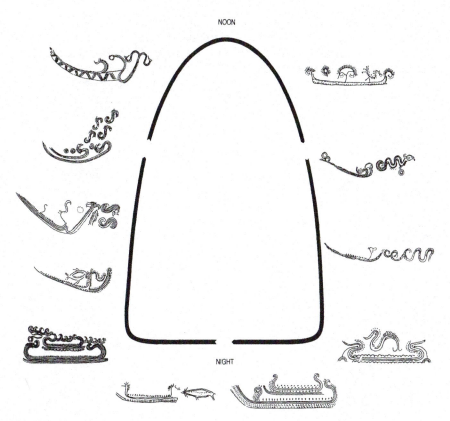

Fig. III.9. Images on Late Bronze Age razors arranged in a probable cosmological sequence. After Kaul 2004.

In the Late Bronze Age, pictures on razors also relate to the travels of the sun (Kaul 2004). The sun drives its horse in daytime travel, but boats also play important roles. No boats sailing towards the left (east) carry the sun, only boats sailing towards the right (west). It has been suggested that the left-sailing boats are the vessels carrying the sun from west to east during its nocturnal journey. A group of animals assisting the sun seems to be part of the myth: fish in the morning (left/east), snake in the evening (right/west). The motifs on razors may even be joined together to form a 'comic-strip'.

A study of the spiral ornaments on female belt-plates, symbolizing the sun and spiked by the tall brimmed hat of the sun-god, has revealed the existence of a calendar system (Randsborg and Christensen 2006). The sum of the ornaments, by applying a simple formula, adds up to the number of days in a particular set of months (see Table 2 on p. 148). The formula is: multiplication by the serial number of the ornamental zone as calculated from the spike.

A similar study of the sun-chariot disc reveals that two different calendars were used: the solar calendar on the day-side and the lunar calendar on the night-side. The Near Eastern 360(+5)-days-to-a-year calendar was also known in the north.

The use of this formula is both simple and advanced. European cultic artefacts also carry day/month numbers, but here it is only a matter of simple arithmetic.

4. Hjortspring Deposit

The Hjortspring boat and weapons deposit of the fourth century BC was found in a tiny bog on the island of Als off South Jylland (Randsborg 1995). It consists of a 19-metre-long double-prowed canoe modelled on Bronze Age vessels. The weight of the canoe, made of knot-free lime, is a mere 500 kg. There are seats for 18 ordinary paddlers; on a small quarter-deck at one end there is ample room for a steersman and two

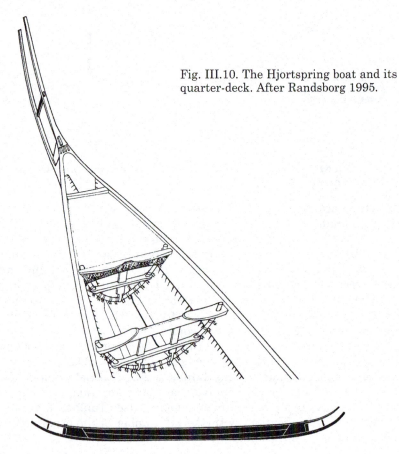

Fig. III.10. The Hjortspring boat and its quarter-deck. After Randsborg 1995.

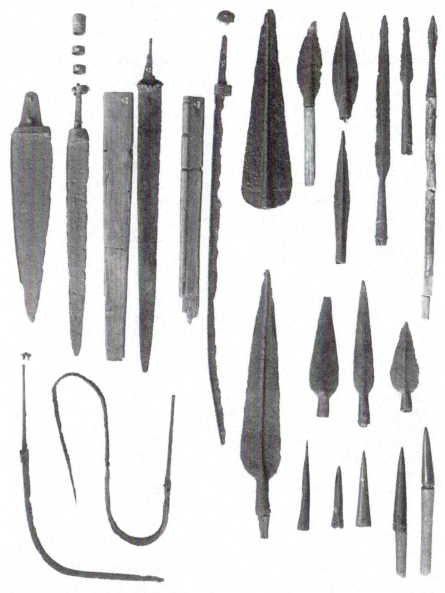

Fig. III.11. Hjortspring weaponry. After Randsborg 1995.

senior warriors; a second steersman and crew-leader were seated at the other end. The free weight allows for additional warriors – perhaps boys – seated between the paddlers. The vessel is surprisingly seaworthy, easy to manoeuvre and very fast; a replica of the boat reaches almost 15 kilometres per hour in sprints, with a daily range of 100-150 kilometres;

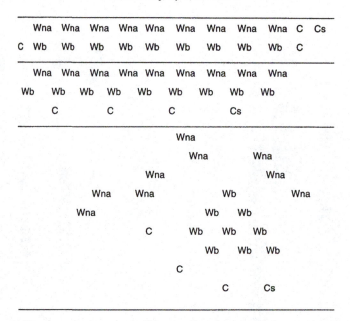

Fig. III.12. Battle techniques possibly employed by the fighters of a Hjortspring unit (spear-boys excluded). C = Commander (sword, bayonet-like lance, narrow shield, mail-coat); W = Common warrior (lance and average shield); n = narrow iron-tipped javelin, b = broad iron-tipped javelin; a = antler/bone-tipped javelin. The front is at the top. After Randsborg 1995.

interestingly, the marching-speed is easily attained with half the paddlers resting. Such canoes must have turned Denmark into a military landscape with constant lookouts. The first sea-barriers, closing off inlets, date to the same archaeological period.

Weaponry is dominated by lances/spears and oblong shields (most are broad, with a few narrow ones likely for senior warriors). Some spears have round antler points, possibly for penetrating chain-mail, which may have been present in the find. There are few swords, probably belonging to senior warriors. In fact, the weaponry found may arm a unit of at least three boats, structurally similar to the contemporary Roman legion: two tiers of spear/lance and shield fighters and a third of 'veterans' with shield, lance and sword, perhaps wearing chain-mail. A front of young *velites* is a possibility.

Among the other objects found are wheel-thrown boxes, which seem to imitate Greek *pyxides* and were copied in clay in an area around Hamburg, possibly the place of origin of the Hjortspring elite corps, perhaps participating in a larger operation: multiple lines of spiked pits (used by Caesar at Alesia) have been found at various places in Jylland. The lines cover many hundreds of metres, indicating opposing armies several thousand soldiers strong.

5. Jelling Complex

The tenth-century royal palace at Jelling in Central Jylland comprises two colossal mounds and two famous rune stones (Randsborg 2008). A drawing was made in the sixteenth century. Archaeological investigations have been ongoing since the early nineteenth century. The North Mound has a Bronze Age mound as its core, into which a richly furnished wooden burial chamber was dug in 959. The South Mound, constructed in the 970s, is empty except for a large stone V, part of a huge ship-setting (centred on the North Mound), 354 metres or 12,000 Roman feet long.

Immediately to the south of the North Mound is a stone church of around 1100 built on top of a series of large wooden churches, among the earliest in Denmark. The oldest – cathedral-sized – church holds a chamber tomb with the bones of a secondary male burial (with artefacts from about 970) who may be King Harald. The church, on the other hand, dates to the 980s.

The smaller rune stone (now next to the large one) was erected by 'King Gorm for his wife Thyra, the adornment (or remedy) of Denmark'. The large second stone was erected by 'King Harald for his father Gorm and his mother Thyra, that Harald who won for himself all of Denmark and Norway and made the Danes Christian'. This stone is decorated with a picture of a fabulous monster fighting a snake above 'Norway' and

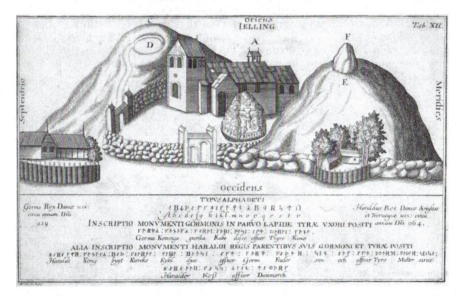

Fig. III.13. Jelling monuments in a wood-cut of the late sixteenth century (cf. Worm 1643-51). After Krogh 1993.

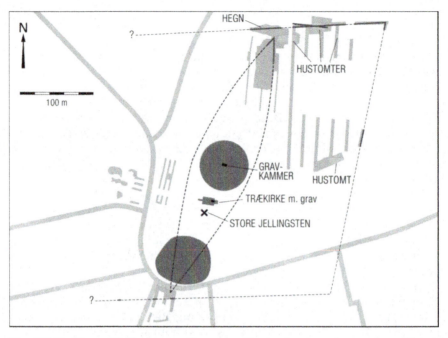

Fig. III.14. Plan of Jelling according to earlier and recent excavations. Note the two huge mounds and the remains of the huge ship-setting. Also marked are the excavation areas and modern roads. [Danish] *Hegn* = fence; *Hustomt(er)* = house structure(s); *Gravkammer* = grave chamber; *Trækirke m. grav* = wooden church w. grave; *Store Jellingsten* = large Jelling [rune] stone. *Ældre hegn* = older fence; *Yngre hegn* = later fence. After Christensen and Andersen 2008. The western side of the palisade fence was located in late 2008, about 100 m to the west of King Harald's rune stone. This find is not included in the figure.

Fig. III.15. King Harald's rune stone. After Wimmer 1893-1908.

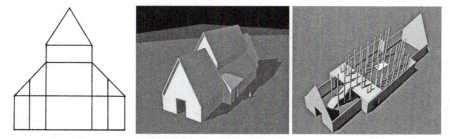

Fig. III.16. The earliest cathedral-sized wooden church at Jelling. After Randsborg 2008.

a depiction of Christ on the cross above 'Christian'. King Harald accepted Christianity in the early 960s.

Recently, the massive palisade fence surrounding the huge palace has been found. The entire ship-setting is within the croft, which also holds a number of halls. A few kilometres to the south of Jelling is a two-lane oak bridge over 700 metres long built in the 980s, likely in connection with the church, which links Jelling with the main north-south road through Jylland.

6. Boringholm Manor House

The fortified wooden Boringholm manor house was built in around 1368 at Rask Sø in East Jylland (Koch and Roesdahl 2005). It represents a new generation of manor houses in wood or stone, detached from villages. The small finds point clearly to the presence of the nobility: elegant shoes, a high percentage of fine glazed pottery, sometimes imported (Germany, France), and high class weapons; even a wooden leg was found. The organic materials are extraordinarily well preserved, with small finds comprising leather accessories (a high 37%), ceramics (15%), other household articles (15%), riding equipment (5%), clothing etc. (4%), weapons (3%), building elements (3%), agricultural tools (3%), other tools (3%), raw materials (3%), items related to transportation (2%), personal belongings (2%), furniture (1%), leisure items (1%) and so on. The meat-based diet was dominated by cattle and sheep; game was common.

The manor house seems to have been abandoned in around 1400, perhaps in response to a general ban on private fortifications issued by Queen Margrete I, the first leader of the Nordic – or Kalmar – Union of 1397. Many fortified manors are known in Jylland, almost all founded in the fourteenth century.

The properties in the area around Boringholm, the district of Nim, are well represented in contemporary written sources; a high 2/3 of farmsteads are recorded, the remainder probably had noble owners, changing the percentages given below (Koch and Roesdahl 2005:

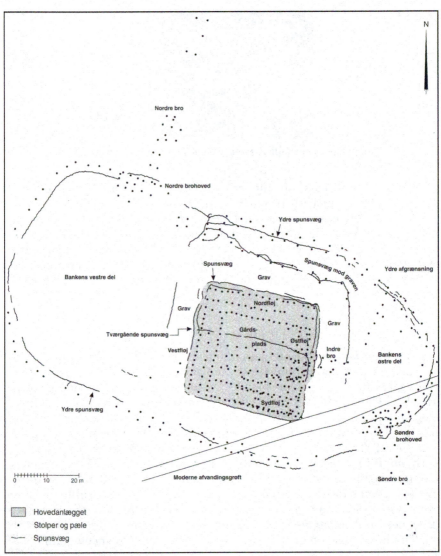

Fig. III.17. Plan of Boringholm manor house: timber walls, bridges and main area of buildings. [Danish] *grav* = moat; *bro* = bridge; *væg* = wall. After Koch and Roesdahl 2005.

267ff./E. Ulsig). In the villages and at other locations, 54 named farms (36%) belonged to the nobility (19% to the high nobility), 37 (25%) to monasteries and churches, and 25 (17%) to the crown; 35 farms (23%) were owned by the farmers themselves. At Boring village, the church owned one farm, the crown three, while one farm was owned by a farmer. Boringholm was first owned by knights, then by the crown (Margrete I, in 1400).

Fig. III.18. Reconstruction of part of the structures at Borlingholm. After Koch and Roesdahl 2005.

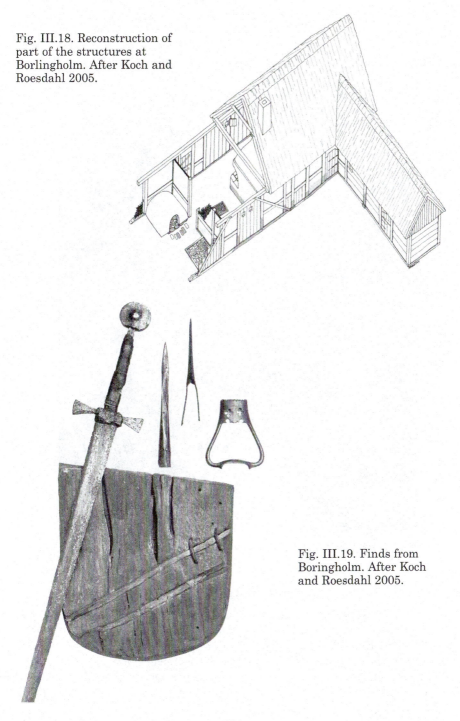

Fig. III.19. Finds from Boringholm. After Koch and Roesdahl 2005.

Fig. III.20. Rosenborg Gateway. After Randsborg 2004.

7. Rosenborg Gateway

Rosenborg in København (1606+) was built by King Christian IV as his small private palace in a large 'pleasure garden' to escape the cramped conditions at København Castle (Randsborg 2004). Christian's sister Anne was Queen of England and Scotland. The two were very close, sharing a love of the arts. Inigo Jones, the famous architect of Queen Anne's Palladian palace at Greenwich of 1616+, visited København in 1603; in 1606 Christian

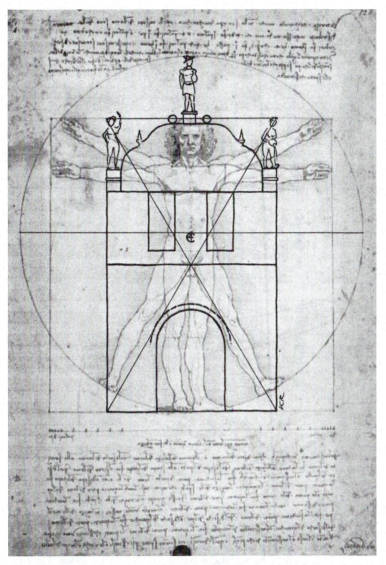

Fig. III.21. The Rosenborg Gateway superimposed on Leonardo da Vinci's 'Vitruvian Man'. After Randsborg 2004.

visited his sister. Their brother Ulrik travelled to England several times; in 1604 he accompanied John Dowland, the famous English composer and musician, to København. In England, Christian IV was attended by Inigo Jones, at the time mainly employed designing costumes and stage sets for the queen's theatrical events. Among his stage sets is a tower with a doorway of 1608, structurally similar to the Rosenborg gateway.

133

Fig. III.22. 'House of Fame' stage set of 1608 by Inigo Jones, for *The Masque of Queens* performed in London in February 1609. After Randsborg 2004.

The gateway (of 1608+) is the only part of the original Rosenborg Palace still visible today. It is a remarkable piece of Renaissance architecture in pink and grey sandstone, adorned with statues and composed according to Vitruvian architectural ideals: buildings as reflections of the proportions of the male body. In fact, the structure fits Leonardo da Vinci's famous 'Vitruvian Man'.

The Rosenborg Gateway, along with many other fine stone structures of the Middle Ages and Renaissance, demonstrates Denmark's desire and ability to adapt to European developments in architecture.

8. Wars with Sweden

King Christian IV engaged Sweden in an unsuccessful war in 1611-13. He next attempted to become the protector of German Protestantism (in opposition to the Catholic Emperor). A decisive battle at Lutter am Barenberge south of Hannover in 1627 led to the Catholic occupation of Jylland. Denmark received fairly mild peace terms, while Sweden continued its expansion; at Lützen near Leipzig in 1632 the Swedish-led Protestant forces won a decisive battle against the Catholic armies. In 1643 Swedish forces suddenly marched into Jylland from the south and into Skåne from Sweden. In 1645 Denmark was forced to cede Halland, along with the Norwegian Jemtland and Herjedalen, for 30 years. Øsel and Gotland in the Baltic were also lost.

Under King Frederik III (1648-70) Denmark declared war on Sweden in 1657. The Swedish army on the continent marched into Jylland and

Fig. III.23. The Swedish army crossing the Danish Belts on the ice in 1658. After Olsen 1988-: vol. 8.

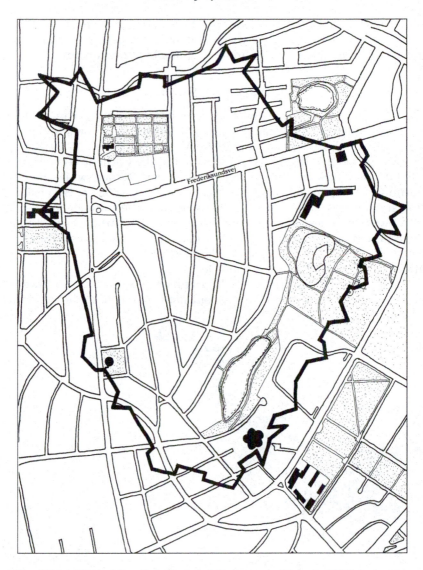

Fig. III.24. Plan of Swedish Karlstad Fortress on Brønshøj Hill just outside København in 1659, superimposed on modern street map. After
Christensen 1996.

during the very cold winter months of 1658 crossed the ice to the Danish
islands, normally protected by the sea and the Danish navy. At the
Peace of Roskilde, Denmark was forced to surrender all its eastern
provinces in addition to Bohus and Trondhjem Len in Norway. The
dukes of Slesvig-Holstein became allies of Sweden. Later in the same
year, the Swedish king decided to capture all of Denmark, landed at

Fig. III.25. Naval battle at Køge Bay (south of København) in 1677. Danish navy squadron of 36 ships against Swedish squadron of 47 ships. Danish losses: 100 dead, two to three times as many wounded; Swedish losses: eight ships-of-the-line plus smaller vessels and 3,000 men. Contemporary medallion. After Olsen 1988-: vol. 8.

Fig. III.26. Admiral P.J. Wessel Tordenskjold – 'Thunder Shield' (1690-1720), terror and scourge of the Swedes, depicted on a modern standard match box. Photo: Author.

Korsør on Sjælland and laid siege to København. The largest Swedish fortification ever – Karlstad – was built on a hill just outside København. The capital received Dutch support and a massive Swedish attack in February 1659 failed completely: Danish losses: 30; Swedish losses: one tenth of the army – the frost was now on the side of Denmark. After the peace of 1660, Trondhjem Len and Bornholm returned to the Danish crown. The population of the lost provinces, especially Skåne, was terrorized; guerrilla warfare continued into the eighteenth century.

The Skåne War followed in 1675-79. Denmark actually reconquered most of its lost provinces, but did not prevail at the negotiating table. The same was true during the Great Nordic War of 1700-20. The only benefit for Denmark was that the dukes of Slesvig-Holstein remained with the crown (and that Sweden became weaker after 1720).

9. Battles with England

In the eighteenth century Denmark benefited greatly from its overseas trade, not least as a neutral power: this represented a problem for England during the Napoleonic Wars. England decided to strike at Denmark in the spring of 1801. To prevent bombard ships from approaching the capital, a line of old ships-of-the-line and some other vessels was formed (the active fleet was not ready after the winter). Admiral H. Nelson onboard the *Elephant* assaulted the Danish line (outnumbered 1:2) south of the Trekroner sea fortress. The battle lasted six hours and resulted in 500 dead and about the same number of

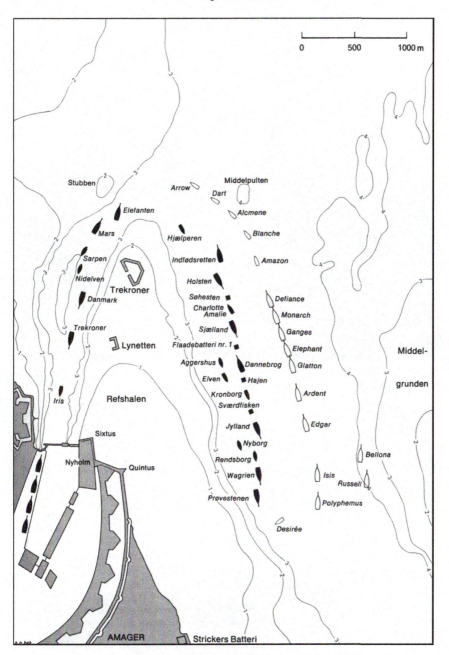

Fig. III.27. Battle of the Roads of København, 2 April 1801, by J.F. Clemens (1748-1831). (*opposite*) Copper-plate engraving of 1802-05. Admiral Nelson (1758-1805) in command of the British ships; Commander Olfert Fischer (1747-1829) of the Danish line. (*above*) Map of the battle, after Feldbæk 1985.

Fig. III.28. København after the bombardment in 1807. Painting of 1808 by J.P. Møller (1783-1854). After Olsen 1988-: vol. 10.

Fig. III.29. Danish gun boats – built after the British bombardment of København in 1807 and the surrender of the Danish fleet – conquering an English brig. Water-colour of 1808 by C.W. Eckersberg (1783-1853). After Olsen 1988-: vol. 10.

wounded on the Danish side (higher numbers are claimed), and 300 dead and twice as many wounded on the British. Nelson threatened to set the captured Danish ships on fire (with the prisoners still onboard), thus forcing a termination of hostilities. Trekroner and the Danish line to the north remained intact, but could not prevent the bombardment of København. At the negotiation table Denmark won respite.

In 1805 Nelson crushed the French-Spanish fleet at Trafalgar. This made the Danish fleet the largest on the continent. In the summer of 1807, England stood alone, threatened with naval blockade and even invasion. It therefore demanded the surrender of the Danish fleet. Virtually the entire Danish army was deployed on the southern border to prevent Napoleon from attacking. English troops laid siege to København, Wellington (the victor at Waterloo) crushed the Sjælland militia and a fire missile bombardment was started that terrorized the capital into surrender. Material damage was substantial and civilian losses high. The capture of the navy put an end to the Double Monarchy, with Norway being ceded to Sweden in 1815.

10. At War with Germany

The First Slesvig War (1848-50) began with a demand for freedom from the Danish crown by the German Slesvig-Holsteiners. The Danish position was that Slesvig – the Danish part of the Duchy – should

Fig. III.30. Storming a German redoubt by N. Simonsen (1807-85): episode during the successful Danish sortie from Fredericia town in July 1849 (at the expense of heavy losses) resulting in German forces abandoning Jylland. After Bruhn 1948.

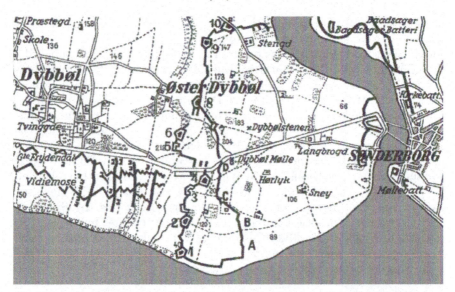

Fig. III.31. The Battle of Dybbøl, 18 April 1864. The defending Danish forces (*right*) were in the numbered fortlets and adjacent trenches. The trenches of the joint forces of Prussia, the Austro-Hungarian Empire, Holstein, and so forth (*left*) zig-zagged towards the Danish lines before the decisive assault. The Danish 8th Brigade counterattack with bayonets (the Danish guns were old-fashioned muzzle loaders) up Dybbøl Hill (at 'Dybbøl Mølle' on the map) cost the lives of 45% of the Danish soldiers present at Dybbøl.

remain part of the kingdom. The German response was to form a Slesvig-Holstein government and army. Denmark easily won the first encounter, but Prussia intervened and several battles followed. In the face of supreme enemy forces, the Danish army withdrew to fortified positions in Jylland in 1849 (while the navy blockaded German harbours). A highly successful sortie was made from the town of Fredericia. Under Russian pressure, Prussia withdrew its forces. The Slesvig-Holstein army was defeated in the largest land battle ever in Scandinavia, at Isted just north of Slesvig City, in 1850. Danish losses were more than 3,000, almost a tenth of the army. After the war, things continued much as before, but Denmark was now a democratic country.

Politicians dreamt of Slesvig as an integrated part of Denmark. In 1863, on the death of King Frederik VII (reign: 1848-63), a new constitution linking Slesvig with Denmark was signed and war commenced with Prussia (led by Bismarck) and the Austro-Hungarian Empire as the main powers supporting the German Slesvig-Holsteiners. The Danish army was in position at Danevirke, but the winter ice, allowing for an enemy attack on its unprotected flank, forced the army to withdraw to a fortified position at Dybbøl, further north. The German forces had far superior weapons and Dybbøl was stormed in April 1864, with terrible losses on the Danish side. The only Danish victories were at sea. Virtually all of Slesvig was lost at the negotiating table, despite English and French support for Denmark.

11. World War II

Denmark was a neutral but armed nation during World War I and thus benefited from participation in international trade, not least that in agricultural products. Between the two wars, Denmark's military forces were severely reduced despite a non-alliance policy. On the outbreak of World War II, Denmark again hoped to stay neutral but was occupied by Germany, along with Norway, on 9 April 1940. Fighting continued in the mountains of Norway for some time, while Denmark accepted the German occupation and started a policy of self-government in collaboration with Germany. A free election was even held in March 1943 (giving the Nazi Party less than 2% of the vote) (see Table 12 on p.

Fig. III.32. Danish war-ships at the naval base in København sunk by their own crews, August 1943. 32 ships were damaged, while one small destroyer, three mine-sweepers and nine cutters escaped to Sweden. After Nørby 2003 (and others).

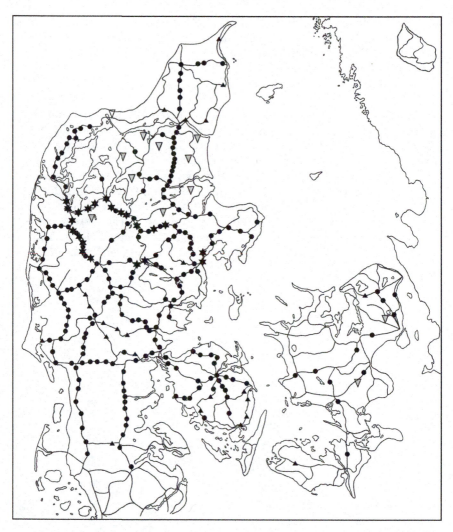

Fig. III.33. Partisan sabotage against railways in Denmark (based on Danish sources, cf. Keegan 1989). Black symbols: triangle = <5 actions; dot = 5-20 actions; star = >20 actions. Open grey triangle = area of British parachute drops of explosives and weapons. Map: Author.

156). However, the government was forced to resign in the summer of 1943, leaving the administration in the hands of the heads of the ministerial offices. On the same day that the government resigned, Danish armed forces managed to sink most of the rather strong navy before being arrested (the air force was destroyed on the ground in 1940). In October 1943 nearly all of Denmark's several thousand Jews were smuggled across to neutral and unoccupied Sweden by the resistance (with tacit help from the German Army). The Danish police force was arrested en masse in 1944 and sent to concentration camps in Germany. The occupation ended on 5 May 1945.

Active resistance had started on a larger scale in 1942 but was suppressed as long as the Danish government continued to function. An underground government, 'The Council of Freedom', was founded when the actual government resigned; in 1944 this body was acknowledged by the Allies. Sabotage increased as British weapons and explosives were air-dropped to the resistance movement. Militarily, the most important actions were sabotage of the railways, particularly in Jylland, facing England and bordering on Germany – the Danish North Sea coast was part of the 'Atlantic Wall' against an Allied invasion. The sabotage of the railways forced the German army to assign large contingents to guard duty and prevented fresh German troops in Norway and Denmark from reaching the fronts towards the end of the war (Fig. III.33).

The resistance movement was an important card in the hands of the Danish government and administrators negotiating with the Germans regarding everyday affairs, since Germany did not wish to have a rebellious Denmark at its rear. Many German civilians fleeing the Russians also found refuge in Denmark. After the war, the active resistance brought Denmark squarely into the allied camp. Denmark's goal – officially and unofficially – was to safeguard the country and prevent a change in its status while occupied.

Tables

Table 1. Archaeological chronology for Denmark
Note the changes in length of the periods

BC	Period	Phenomena	Europe & World
14000			
	Hamburg Culture		
12000	Federmesser Culture		
	Bromme Culture		
10000	Ahrensburg Culture	End of the Ice Age	
	Early Maglemose Culture		Domesticates in Near East
8000	– Middle		
	– Late		
6000	Kongemose Culture		Villages in Turkey
	Early Ertebølle Culture		Farmers in Central Europe
5000	– Middle	Kitchen middens	
	– Late		Copper Age in Bulgaria
4000	Early Neolithic	Domesticates & plough	
	Middle Neolithic	Dolmens & passage graves	Ötzi*; towns in Near East
3000	Single-grave cultures	Wagons	
	Late Neolithic		Pyramids in Egypt
2000			Palaces in Greece
	Early Bronze Age	Chariots/aristocracy/sun-cult	
1000	Late Bronze Age		City-states in Greece
			Iron Age in Central Europe
500	Celtic Iron Age	War canoes	Greek colonies
			Alexander the Great
0	Roman Iron Age	Villages	Roman Empire
		Rowing ships	
500	Migration Period		Frankish Kingdom
		Sailing ships	Rise of Islam
750	Viking Age	Nordic expansion	Charlemagne
		Kings of Denmark	
1000		Churches & towns	European nations
	Middle Ages	Absalon	Crusades
1250		Castles	Decline of Byzantium
	– Nordic Union	Commerce	Gun-powder
1500	Renaissance	Manor houses	Columbus
	Baroque	Loss of Skåne	Absolutism
1750	Enlightenment	Agricultural reforms	World commerce
	Democracy	Industrial production	National rivalry
2000	New challenges	Information society	World encounters

*Ötzi is the nickname of the man found in glacier ice in the Ötz Valley, on the border between Austria and Italy.

Table 2

Calendrically significant numbers hidden in the decoration of Early Bronze Age artefacts emerging from multiplications: the sun-chariot from Trundholm Bog, Sjælland and the belt-plate from Langstrup Bog, Sjælland, both from the fourteenth century BC.

Sun-chariot

(A) Day-side
9 ornaments in the first zone (beyond the centre), 16 in the second and 27 in the third. Or 9 x 1 plus 16 x 2 plus 27 x 3 = 122.
122 = 4 (Sun) months in days (1 month = 30.5 days).
(B) Night-side
1 ornament in the first zone (the centre), 8 in the second, 20 in the third and 25 in the fourth. Or 1 x 1 plus 8 x 2 plus 20 x 3 plus 25 x 4 = 177.
177 = 6 (Moon) months in days. (1 month = 29.5 days.)

Langstrup belt-plate

Multiplication as in (A) above
Sum of multiplied ornaments = 265.
265 = 9 (Moon) months in days. (1 month = 29.5 days.)
265 = Length of women's pregnancy.
Multiplication as in (B) above
Sum of multiplied ornaments = 360.
360 = 12 (Near Eastern) months in days, or one year.
The remaining 5 (extra) days may be depicted as the 5 bundles of lines on the point.

Table 3. Danish house types, 1000-1200 AD
data from Skov 1994

	1000	1025	1050	1075	1100	1125	1150	1175
Three-aisled	70	54	32	22	4	3	3	4
Oblique braces*	22	10	10	8	2	1	1	0
Two-aisled	4	6	9	10	6	6	7	10
One-aisled	11	14	39	42	47	45	34	35
Stone-based*	1	1	1	1	6	6	8	9
Projection-house*	0	0	3	4	7	8	8	9
Σ	*108*	*85*	*94*	*87*	*72*	*69*	*61*	*67*
Pit-houses	35	25	20	17	9	3	1	2
ΣΣ	*143*	*110*	*114*	*104*	*81*	*72*	*62*	*69*

*One-aisled

149

Anatomy of Denmark

Table 4

Top: Medieval parish churches in Denmark (cf. Map 2): the vast majority were founded in the Romanesque period (after Wienberg 1993). There is a strong correlation between soil quality and number of churches, indicating that the latter are valid population measures. There were 300-400 adults per church/parish. *Middle:* Romanesque town churches in cities and towns (after Andrén 1985). A smaller number of the churches in towns with only one church are Gothic; however, these probably had predecessors, even in wood. *Bottom:* Information from the Icelandic *Knytlinge Saga* of the early thirteenth century on the numbers of churches and 'ships' (units of land) in the dioceses of Denmark (Bekker-Nielsen 1977: Book 32): a correlation is noted between the two.

Dioceses	Churches
Børglum (North Jylland)	197
Viborg (North Central Jylland)	265
Århus (East Jylland)	392
Ribe (West Jylland)	313
Slesvig (South Jylland)	216 (some now under the North Sea)
Odense (Fyn & Islands; Lolland, Falster, Femern)	322
Roskilde (Sjælland, Møn)	412
Lund (Skåne & Bornholm, Halland, Blekinge)	575 (or 21%, also without Bornholm)
Σ	2692

Cities (1-22 churches)	Main towns (2-4 churches)	Other towns (1 church)
Børglum 1	Hjørring 3	
Viborg 12-14	Ålborg 3; Skive 2	
Århus 3	Randers 4; Horsens 2	
Ribe 6	Varde 2; Tønder 2	
Slesvig 8	Flensborg 3	
Odense 3	Svendborg 2	
Roskilde 14	Slagelse 4; København 4; Kalundborg 2;	
	Næstved 2; Vordingborg 2; Holbæk 2;	
	Ringsted 2; Slangerup 2	
Lund 22	Helsingborg 4; Ystad 2; Tommarp 2	
Σ 69-71	Σ 51	Σ 85
		(inc. ≥19 Gothic ones)

Dioceses	Churches	'Ships'
Hjørring (North Jylland)	150	50
Viborg	250	100
Århus	200	90
Ribe	324	120
Hedeby (Slesvig)	350	130
Odense	300	100
Roskilde	411	120
Lund	353	150
Σ	2,338	860

Notes: Bornholm has 16 churches. Børglum is a village in northern Jylland. *Knytlinge Saga* gives Hjørring for Børglum and Hedeby for Slesvig. It also gives Bornholm 14 churches (and '12 royal farms').

Table 5. Structure of medieval and later villages: distribution of rent in grain and area of arable land

A decline in population is assumed for the later Middle Ages, as is an emphasis on animal husbandry, less demanding of labour and supported by abandoned arable land. In Horns District alone, with high quality arable land, 8 villages were abandoned, leaving one of the churches without its village (Olsen 1988-: vol.6; Dahlerup: 79f.). The deterioration of the climate from the fourteenth century onwards caused problems for agriculture. *Top:* The village of Hørve, Sjælland. Payment of rent to the owner is in barrels of grain in the years 1290, *c.* 1370 and 1591. There is a clear move towards smaller farms of more equal size; however, the original 12 farms can also be traced through time. Payments of other kinds of rent, in particular work on the main farms by copy-holders (cf. the year 1290), or even on nearby Dragsholm Manor (early thirteenth century), are not included. *Middle:* The village of Farum, Sjælland. Amount of land belonging to farms in terms of 'barrels of hard corn' (the amount of barley used to sow a certain area) *c.* 1370 and 1682. The copy-holders of *c.* 1370, like the farmers of 1682, also worked on the main farm. Here too, a development towards the standardization of farm sizes is noted. *Below:* Kasted, Jylland. Payment of rent in barrels of grain in the years 1315, *c.* 1415 and post-1500.

Hørve 1290

Farms	Rent	Σ
3	48+48+48	144
3	28+24+24	76
6*	0+0+0+0+0+0	0
Σ12		220

Hørve c. 1370

Farms	Rent	Σ
1	48	48
2	36+36	72
2	24+24	48
1	12	12
3	6+6+6	18
3	4+4+4	12
Σ12		210

Hørve 1591

Farms	Rent	Σ
1	20	20
4	12+10+10+10	42
7	8+8+6+6+6+6+6	46
9	2+2+2+2+2+2+2+2+2	18
Σ21		126

Farum 1290

Farms	Land	Σ
?	?	

Farum c. 1370

Farms	Land	Σ
1	51	51
30	~2.8 each	84
Σ31		135

Farum 1682

Farms	Land	Σ
1	17	17
19	~6.2 each	118
Σ20		135

Kasted 1315

Farms	Rent	Σ
1	49½	49½
3	1½+1½+1½	4½
Σ4		54

Kasted c. 1415

Farms	Rent	Σ
?	?	18
		18

Kasted 1500+

Farms	Rent	Σ
4	~6	24
Σ4		24

*Plus 1 vacant

Table 6. Foundation dates of medieval Danish towns.

Note the decline in foundations in the late fourteenth century, corresponding with the decline in rural settlement, and the Black Death of *c*. 1350 and later (cf. Table 5) (data from Hybel and Poulsen 2007; mainly based on Andrén 1985). In the 1200-1350 group, 18 of the new towns are on Sjælland (and the islands) but only 8 in Skåne. Note the late urban development of small but wealthy Fyn and of the marginal provinces of East Denmark.

	1000-1200	1200-1350	1350-1400	1400-1550	Σ
Jylland	9	17	0	12	38
Fyn (& Islands)	1	9	0	1	11
Sjælland (& Islands) & Skåne	10	26	0	9	45
Halland, Bornholm & Blekinge	0	11	0	9	20
Σ	20	63	0	31	114

Table 7. Shifting attitudes to crime and punishment through the ages (Olsen 1988-: vol. 16)

The punishments mentioned are maximum penalties; nowadays especially a substantial percentage of offenders are pardoned. One mark silver was equivalent to 200+ grams. The death penalty was only rarely applied in the nineteenth century and since then has been used in only a few cases of high treason during World War II. The penalties of the High Middle Ages seem light compared to the early days of the absolute monarchy; democratic Denmark only gradually lessened punishments. Note that assault, robbery and in particular rape – an attack on a person – is still heavily punished.

Law code	Jylland 1241	Denmark 1683	Penalty 1866	Penalty 1930	Penalty 2003
Crimes					
Witchcraft	–	Burning	–	–	–
Lèse-majesté	–	Right hand cut off, body quartered, put on wheel, head on stake	Penal servitude ≤8 years	–	–
Homicide	Fine of 18 Mark	Execution, loss of property	Execution or penal servitude 8 years to life	Prison 5 years to life	Prison 5 years to life
Serious assault	Outlawed or payment of fine	Chain-work for life at naval dock	Work at fortress or open prison, ¾-4 years	Fine, open prison, or prison <2 years	Fine, open prison, or prison ≤6 years
Full rape	Outlawed	Execution	Prison for life or ≥4 years penal servitude	Prison ≤16 years	Prison ≤12 years
Minor theft	Fine of 3 Mark, branding	Whipping	Hard prison ≥5 days	Prison ≤2 years	Prison ≤1½ years
Large theft	Hanging	Whipping & branding	Penal servitude ≤8 years	Prison ≤6 years	Prison ≤4 years
Robbery	Fine of 3 Mark	Execution, body on wheel	Penal servitude ≤10 years	Prison 6-10 years	Prison ≤6 years

Table 8. Towns in today's Denmark by 1769

Towns with more than 1000 inhabitants are marked with *s per 1000, except huge **København**. The capital is by far the largest city, followed by Odense on Fyn, Ålborg in North Jylland, Århus in East Jylland, Helsingør on Sjælland and Haderslev in South Jylland. Danish Flensborg in South Slesvig had 10,700 inhabitants in 1803.

Jylland (without South Slesvig)

Skagen 700
Hjørring 600
Sæby 500
****Ålborg 4400 (*****5600 in 1801)
*Nibe 1000 (1000 in 1801)
Thisted 800 (*1100 in 1801)
Nykøbing Mors 600
Hobro 500
Mariager 400
Randers 2900 (**4600 in 1801)
Grenå 700
Æbeltoft 600
Viborg 2200 (2400 in 1801)
Skive 400
Århus 3800 (*4000 in 1801)

Skanderborg 600
Horsens 2700 (2400 in 1801)
*Vejle 1000 (*1300 in 1801)
Fredericia 2800 (*3500 in 1801)
*Kolding 1500 (*1700 in 1801)
Lemvig 300
Holstebro 700
Ringkøbing 500
Varde 900 (*1000 in 1801)
Ribe 2100 (2000 in 1801)
Haderslev 3100 (3600 in 1803)
Åbenrå 2700 (2800 in 1803)
Sønderborg 2700 (2800 in 1803)
Tønder 2600 (2600 in 1803)

Fyn and islands

*****Odense 5500 (*****5800 in 1801)
Kerteminde 700 (*1000 in 1801)
Bogense 400
Middelfart 700 (*1000 in 1801)
*Assens 1100 (*1400 in 1801)
*Nyborg 1600 (*1900 in 1801)

*Fåborg 1100 (*1100 in 1801)
*Svendborg 1800 (*1900 in 1801)
*Ærøskøbing 1100 (*1300 in 1801)
Marstal 800 (*1400 in 1801)
Rudkøbing 800 (*1100 in 1801)

Sjælland and islands

Helsingør 3700 (**5300 in 1801)
*Hillerød 1100 (*1200 in 1801)
Slangerup 400
København 71,000 (101,000 in 1801)
*Roskilde 1700 (*1800 in 1801)
Frederikssund 200
*Køge 1400 (*1500 in 1801)
Nykøbing Sjælland 500
*Holbæk 1200 (*1300 in 1801)
*Kalundborg 1300 (*1300 in 1801)
*Korsør 1400 (*1200 in 1801)
Skelskør 600
*Slagelse 1400 (*1700 in 1801)
Sorø 500

Ringsted 700
*Næstved 1400 (*1800 in 1801)
Store Heddinge 500
Præstø 400
Vordingborg 800
*Nakskov 1300 (*1700 in 1801)
Maribo 500
Sakskøbing 400
Rødby 700
Nysted 500
*Nykøbing Falster 1000 (*1100 in 1801)
Stubbekøbing 500
Stege 800

Table 8 (contd.)

Bornholm

Rønne 2100 (2400 in 1801)
Hasle 400
Allinge 300
Sandvig 200

Svaneke 600
Neksø *1200 (*1300 in 1801)
Åkirkeby 400

Table 9. Percentage of the population living in towns
Olsen 1988-: vol. 11; K. Hvidt

	Denmark	Norway	Sweden	England
1800	21	9	10	34
1850	21	13	11	54
1870	25	17	13	65
1900	38	28	22	78

Table 10

Numbers of various types of homes and holdings, their collective amount of land as measured in barrels of hard corn (barley) and the average amount of land/productivity per holding in 1885 (after Olsen 1988-: vol. 11; K. Hvidt).

	Number	%	Barrels	%	Barrels/holding
Manor houses	900	0.3	40,000	11	44
Farms	73,000	28	290,000	78	4
Small-holdings	188,000	72	40,000	11	0.2
Σ	261,900		370,000		[1.4]

Table 11

Development of residential houses in terms of size, average number of inhabitants and key facilities during the twentieth century (after Olsen 1988-: vol. 16); only the provincial towns are listed for the year 1911.

Year	1911	1930	1950	1970	1988
Houses (no. of main rooms)					
One room (%)	7	5	6	4	4
Two rooms (%)	38	35	37	21	18
Three rooms (%)	30	28	29	28	24
Four rooms (%)	12	16	16	25	27
Five rooms or more (%)	13	16	12	22	27
Inhabitants per residence	4.0	3.3	3.0	2.7	2.3
Facilities					
Central heating (%)	–	10	35	84	92
Water closet (%)	–	57	83	96	96
Bath with hot & cold water (%)	–	16	38	77	86

Table 12. Free elections to the Danish Parliament in March 1943: numbers of votes and seats

The Communist Party was banned by German dictate; the party of the German minority in Slesvig did not run. Note the very low number of votes for the Nazi Party despite the German occupation (1940-45), a surprise and embarrassment to Germany. Until the break with Germany in 1943, the Social Democratic and Radical Liberal parties formed the Danish government.

Parties	Votes	Seats	Seats in 1939
Communist	–	–	3
Social Democratic	895,000	66	64
Radical Liberal	175,000	13	14
Liberal (Georgism)	31,000	2	3
Liberal	377,000	28	30
Conservative	422,000	31	26
Danish Unity	43,000	3	0
Farmers	25,000	2	0
German (Slesvig)	–	–	1
Nazi	43,000	3	3

Table 13. Denmark's Economy

Key figures *c.* 2005 unless otherwise indicated. GNP = Gross National Product. M = 1000. Applied Exchange Rate: 1 US$ = 6 Danish Kroner (DKK). Actual Exchange Rate of 2008: 1 US$ = substantially less than 5 DKK and falling.

GNP, purchasing power = $214MMM (2008)
GNP, currency value = $332MMM (2008)
GNP, growth rate = 1.5% (2008)
GNP, per person = $40M (2008)
GNP, Agriculture = 1.5%, Industry = 25%, Services = 74%
Workforce = 2.9MM (Agriculture 4%, Industry 17%, Services 79%)
Unemployment = 4% (2008: below 2%)
Inflation = 2%
Investment = 20% of GNP
State Budget = $149MMM (income); $143MMM (expenses); Defence = $3.2MMM
State Debt = $100MMM
Industrial Production, growth rate = 4%
Electricity, production = 43MMM kWh (fossil fuel 80%; wind 20% and growing)
Electricity, consumption = 32MMM kWh
Electricity, export = 16MMM kWh
Electricity, import = 7MMM kWh
Oil Production = 377M barrels/day
Oil Consumption = 188M barrels/day
Oil Export = 332M barrels/day
Oil Import = 195M barrels/day
Oil Reserves, known = 1.2 MMM barrels
Natural Gas, production = 8.4MMMm^3
Natural Gas, consumption = 5.3MMMm^3
Natural Gas, export = 3.1MMM m^3 (no import)
Natural Gas, known reserves = 82MMMm^3
Balance of Payment = $7MMM (positive)
Export = $85MMM (Germany 18%, Sweden 13%, Great Britain 9%, USA 6%, Netherlands 6%, Norway 5%, France 5%)
Import = $75MMM (Germany 22%, Sweden 14%, Netherlands 7%, Great Britain 6%, France 5%, Norway 5%, Italy 4%, China 4%)
Reserves, foreign currency & gold = $40MMM
Total Debt, including private sector = $405MMM
Economic Support, developing countries (DANIDA) = $1.6MMM
Income Tax, often = 50%; VAT = 25%; property taxes etc. should be added to this figure.

Bibliography

Danish prehistory is covered in detail in Jensen 2001-; historical periods in particular in Olsen 1988-. Both of these major works are in Danish but have numerous illustrations. The Skåne provinces are not covered by Jensen and are dealt with only to a limited extent by Olsen. A short supplement covering these provinces is Johannesson 1981, in particular for later centuries. Notably, Danish archaeological and historical guidebooks now comprise both southern Slesvig and the Skåne provinces. This allows for the integration of the isolated island of Bornholm in the Baltic. It also allows the southernmost part of Scandinavia – 'Old Denmark' – to be seen as the cultural unit it has been throughout history and still is today.

Scarre 2005 outlines the world stage of archaeology in English; unfortunately, the chapter on Europe is rather weak. An older work of similar scope is A. Sherratt 1980. European archaeological surveys in English are somewhat outdated but still useful (e.g. Champion, Gamble, Shennan and Whittle 1984). Renfrew and Bahn 1991 is more of a textbook, primarily aimed at the American market.

A few outdated shorter accounts in English on 'Danish History' are mainly aimed at tourists and virtually omit earlier periods. Works on European history make little reference to Denmark and Scandinavia, except when these countries play a role in the history of major powers, for instance during the Viking Age or during major wars, including World War II. The Scandinavian welfare state of recent times has also attracted attention for its organization and balance between a strong public sector and a strong capitalist economy (to provide revenue).

The works below are mainly scientific studies substantiating the contents of the present volume; a fair number are also quoted in the text. Finally, Wikipedia may also be helpful to the reader.

Aaris-Sørensen, K. (1988), *Danmarks forhistoriske dyreverden. Fra Istid til Vikingetid* (København: Gyldendal).

Adam = Adam of Bremen = Lund, A.A. (ed.) (2000), *Adam af Bremens krønike* (Højbjerg: Wormianum).

Albrethsen, S.E. and Petersen, E.B. (1976), 'Excavation of a Mesolithic Cemetery at Vedbæk, Denmark', *Acta Archaeologica* 47: 1ff.

Andersen, H.H. (1998), *Danevirke og Kovirke. Arkæologiske undersøgelser 1861-1993* (Højbjerg: Jysk Arkæologisk Selskab/Aarhus Universitetsforlag).

Andersen, H.H. (2004), *Til hele rigets værn*, (Højbjerg: Moesgaard & Wormianum).

Andersen, N.H. (1997-99), *The Sarup Enclosures 1-3. The Funnel Beaker Culture of the Sarup Site Including Two Causewayed Camps Compared to the Contemporary Settlements in the Area and Other European Enclosures* (Højbjerg: Jysk Arkæologisk Selskab, Moesgaard/Aarhus University Press).

Andersen, S.H. (1986), 'Mesolithic Dug-outs and Paddles from Tybrind Vig, Denmark', *Acta Archaeologica* 57: 87ff.

Bibliography

Andersson, M., Karsten, P., Knarrström, B. and Svensson, M. (2004), *Stone Age Scania. Significant Places Dug and Read by Contract Archaeology* (Lund: National Heritage Board. Archaeological Excavations, UV Syd).

Andrén, A. (1985), *Den urbana scenen. Städer och samhälle i det medeltida Danmark* (Bonn/Malmö: Habelt/Gleerup).

Ambrosiani, B. and Clarke, H. (eds) (1995), *Excavations in the Black Earth 1990* (Stockholm: Riksantikvarieämbetet & Statens Historiska Museer).

Asingh, P. and Lynnerup, N. (eds) (2007), *Grauballe Man: An Iron Age Bog Body Revisited* (Højbjerg: Moesgaard Museum/Jutland Archaeological Society/Aarhus University Press).

Bar-Yosef, O. (ed.) (2004), 'Agricultural Origins and Dispersal into Europe', *Current Anthropology* 45: 1ff.

Bekker-Nielsen, H. et al. (eds) (1977), *Knytlinge Saga. Knud den Stores, Knud den Hellige. Deres Mænd, deres Slægt* (København: Gad).

Birkebæk, F. (1982), *Danmarkshistorien. Vikingetiden 1. Rejselystne bønder* (København: Sesam).

Boye, V. (1896), *Fund af Egekister fra Bronzealderen i Danmark. Et monografisk Bidrag til Belysning af Bronzealderens Kultur* (Kjøbenhavn: Høst; 1986 reprint Højbjerg: Wormianum).

Bjerg, H.C. and Frantzen O.L. (2005), *Danmark i krig* (København: Politiken).

Brinch Petersen, E. (1974), 'Gravene ved Dragsholm. Fra jægere til bønder for 6000 år siden', *Nationalmuseets Arbejdsmark*: 112ff.

Bruhn, A. (1948), *Et Hundredaarsminde om Treaarskrigen* (København: Berlingske).

Carelli, P. (2001), *En kapitalistisk anda. Kulturelle förändringar i Danmark i 1100-tallets Danmark* (Stockholm: Almqvist & Wiksell).

Champion, T., Gamble, C., Shennan, S. and Whittle, A. (1984), *Prehistoric Europe* (London: Academic).

Chikhi, L., Nichols, R.A., Barbujani, G. and Beaumont, M.A. (2002), 'Y Genetic Data Support the Neolithic Demic Diffusion Model', *Proceedings of the National Academy of Sciences* 99/17: 11008-13.

Christensen, A.E. (1938), 'Danmarks Befolkning i Middelalderen' in Schück 1938, 1ff.

Christensen, A.E. (1969), *Vikingetidens Danmark. Paa oldhistorisk baggrund* (København: Historisk Institut, Københavns Universitet/Gyldendal).

Christensen, P. Mohr and Andersen, S.W. (2008), 'Kongeligt?', *Skalk* 1: 3ff.

Christensen, P. Thorning (1996), *Guide til Københavns Befæstning. 900 års befæstningshistorie* (København: Miljø- og Energiministeriet/Skov- og Naturstyrelsen).

Cinthio, M. (2004), 'Trinitatiskyrkan, gravarna och de första lundaborna', in Lund 2004, 159ff.

Cook, R. (gen. ed.) (2006), *Wallpaper City Guides: Copenhagen* (London: Phaidon).

Cramer-Petersen, L. (1997), *Carlstad. Københavns naboby 1658-60. En billedfortælling om Svenskekrigene 1657-60 og om svenskernes befæstede lejr i Brønshøj-Carstad* (Brønshøj: Brønshøj Museum).

Damm, A. (ed.) (2005), *Vikingernes Aros* (Højbjerg: Moesgård Museum).

Dahlerup, T. (1989), *De fire stænder. Gyldendals og Politikens Danmarkshistorie 6* (København: Gyldendal & Politiken).

Dehn, T., Hansen, S.I. and Kaul, F. (1995), *Kong Svends Høj. Restaureringer og undersøgelser på Lolland 1991. Stenaldergrave i Danmark 1* (København: Nationalmuseet/Skov- og Naturstyrelsen).

Bibliography

Dehn, T., Hansen, S.I. and Kaul, F. (2000), *Klekkendehøj og Jordehøj. Restaureringer og undersøgelser 1985-90. Stenaldergrave i Danmark 2* (København: Nationalmuseet/Skov- og Naturstyrelsen).

Dehn, T. and Hansen, S.I. (2000), 'Tæt og tørt', *Skalk* 5: 27ff.

Diamond, J. (2005), *Guns, Germs, and Steel: The Fates of Human Societies* (New York: Norton).

Einarsson, L. (2001), *Kronan* (Kalmar: County Museum).

Engberg, N. and Frandsen, J. (2006), 'Engelsborg – et befæstet orlogsværft på Slotø i Nakskov Fjord', *Nationalmuseets Arbejdsmark*: 115ff.

Ersgård, L. (1988), *'Vår Marknad i Skåne'. Bebyggelse, handel och urbanisering i Skanör och Falsterbo under medeltiden* (Lund: Almqvist & Wiksell International).

Ethelberg, P. et al. (2000), *Skovgårde. Ein Bestattungsplatz mit reichen Frauengräbern des 3. Jhs. n.Chr. auf Seeland* (København: Det Kongelige Nordiske Oldskriftselskab/Lynge).

Ethelberg, P., Jørgensen, E., Meier, D. and Robinsen, D. (2000), *Det sønderjyske landbrugs historie. Sten- og Bronzealder* (Haderslev: Haderslev Museum & Historisk Samfund for Sønderjylland).

Ethelberg, N. Hardt, Poulsen, B. and Sørensen, A.B. (2003), *Det sønderjyske landbrugs historie. Jernalder, vikingetid og middelalder* (Haderslev: Haderslev Museum & Historisk Samfund for Sønderjylland).

Feldbæk, O. (1985), *Slaget på Reden* (København: Politiken).

Feveile, C. (ed.) (2006), *Ribe studier. Det ældste Ribe. Udgravninger på nordsiden af Ribe Å 1984-2000* (Højbjerg/Ribe: Jysk Arkæologisk Selskab/Aarhus Universitetsforlag & Den antikvariske Samling).

de Fine Licht, K. and Michelsen, V. (eds) (1988-89), *Danmarks Kirker* (Herning: Kristensen).

Frederiksen, H.J. and Kolstrup, I.-L. (1993), *Ny dansk kunsthistorie 1. Troens kunst* (København: Fogtdal).

Friis-Johansen, K. (1923), 'Hoby-Fundet', *Nordiske Fortidsminder* 2: 3 (Kjøbenhavn: Thiele).

From, I. and Jensen, L.K. (eds) (2003), *Anton Rosen. Arkitekt og Kunstner/Architect and Artist* (Silkeborg: KunstCentret Silkeborg Bad).

Graham-Campbell, J. and Valor, M. (eds) (2007), *The Archaeology of Medieval Europe*, vol. 1: *Eighth to Twelfth Centuries AD* (Aarhus: Aarhus University Press).

Græbe, H., Als Hansen, B. and Stiesdal, H. (1990), 'Gundsømagle kirke. En bygningshistorisk undersøgelse', *Nationalmuseets Arbejdsmark*: 141ff.

Grimm, H. (1977), 'Informationsgewinn am Skelett. Anthropologie und Medizin als Hilfswissenschaften der Archäologie', in Herrmann 1977: 493ff.

Hansen, P. Birk. (2003), 'Boderne i Næstved – middelalderlig boligkultur i praksis', in Roesdahl (ed.): 193ff.

Hansen, S. (1995), 'Tvillingsten', *Skalk* 5: 16ff.

Hårdh, B. and Larsson, L. (2007), *Uppåkra – Lund före Lund* (Lund: Gamla Lund).

Haastrup, U. and Egevand, R. (eds) (1986), *Danske kalkmalerier. Romansk tid. 1080-1175* (København: Nationalmuseet).

Hedegaard, E.O.A. (1970 [2007]), *Krigen på Sjælland* (Helsingør: Andersen).

Herrmann, J. (ed.) (1977), *Archäologie als Geschichtwissenschaft, Studien und Untersuchungen* (Berlin: Akademie).

Hoffmann, E. (1984), 'Beiträge zur Geschichte der Beziehungen zwischen dem

161

deutschen und dem dänischen Reich für die Zeit von 934 bis 1035', in Radtke and Körber (eds): 105ff.

Holm, H.J., Kock, O.V. and Storck, H. (eds) (1894), *Tegninger af ældre nordisk Architektur III:2* (Kjøbenhavn: Hagerup).

Høyer, K. Rosenkrans (ed.) (1988), *Boderne i Næstved* (Næstved: Næstved Kommune/Miljøministeriet Planstyrelsen).

Hübner, E. (2005), *Jungneolithische Gräber auf der Jütischen Halbinsel: Typologische und chronologische Studien zur Einzelgrabkultur I-III* (København: Det Kongelige nordiske Oldskriftselskab).

Hvass, L. (1980), *Danmarkshistorien. Jernalderen 1. Landsbyen og samfundet* (København: Sesam).

Hvass, S. (1985), *Hodde. Et vestjysk landsbysamfund fra ældre jernalder* (København: Akademisk).

Hvass, S. (1986), 'Vorbasse. Eine Dorfsiedlung während des 1. Jahrtausends n.Chr. in Mitteljütland, Dänemark', *Berichte der römisch-germanische Kommission* 67: 529ff.

Hvass, S. (1988), 'Jernalderens bebyggelse', in Mortensen and Rasmussen: 53ff.

Hvidt, K. (1990), *Det folkelige gennembrud og dets mænd. 1850-1900. Politikens og Gyldendal Danmarkshistorie 11* (København: Politiken & Gyldendal).

Hybel, N. (2003), *Danmark i Europa 750-1300* (København: Tusculanum).

Hybel, N. and Poulsen, B. (2007), *The Danish Resources c. 1000-1550. Growth and Recession. The Northern World. North Europe and the Baltic c. 400-1700 AD* (Leiden: Brill).

Ilkjær, J. (2000), *Illerup Ådal. Et arkæologisk tryllespejl* (Højbjerg: Moesgaard).

Ingesmand, P. and Jensen, J.V. (eds) (1994), *Danmark i Senmiddelalderen* (Aarhus: Aarhus Universitetsforlag).

Iversen, M. (ed.) (1991), *Mammen. Grav, kunst og samfund i vikingetid* (Højbjerg: Jysk Arkæologisk Selskab/Aarhus Universitetsforlag).

Jakobsen, T.B. et al. (2007), 'Birth of a World Museum', *Acta Archaeologica* 78:1.

Jensen, B. (2003), *Moderne gennembrud i Aalborg i 1930erne. Aalborgbogen 2003* (Aalborg: Selskabet for Aalborgs historie).

Jensen, J. (1998), *Manden i kisten. Hvad bronzealderens gravhøje gemte* (København: Gyldendal).

Jensen, J. (2001-), *Danmarks Oldtid I-IV* (København: Gyldendal).

Jespersen, S. (1947), 'Nationalmuseets Bondegaardsundersøgelser', *Nationalmuseets Arbejdsmark* 1947: 11ff.

Johannsen, H. (ed.) (1983), *Kirkens bygning og brug. Studier tilegnet Elna Møller* (København: Nationalmuseet).

Johannsen, H. and Smidt, C.M. (1981), *Danmarks Arkitektur. Kirkens huse* (København: Gyldendal).

Johannesson, G. (1981), *Danmarks historie – uden for Danmark. Skåne, Halland og Blekinge* (København: Politiken).

Jørgensen, L. (2003), 'Manor and market at Lake Tissø in the sixth to eleventh centuries: the Danish "productive" sites', in Pestell and Ulmschneider: 175ff.

Jørgensen, L., Storgaard, B. and Thomsen, L.G. (eds) (2003), *The Spoils of Victory: The North in the Shadow of the Roman Empire* (København: Nationalmuseet).

Kaul, F. (1989), 'Klekkendehøj og Jordehøj. 5000-årige ingeniørarbejder', *Nationalmuseets Arbejdsmark* 1989: 85ff.

Kaul, F. (1995), 'The Gundestrup Cauldron Reconsidered', *Acta Archaeologica* 66: 1ff.

Kaul, F. (2004), *Bronzealderens religion. Studier af den nordiske bronzealder ikonografi* (København: Det kongelige Nordiske Oldskriftselskab).

Karsten, P. and Knarrström, B. (eds) (2001), *Skånska spår – arkeologi längs Västkustbanan. Tågerup. Specialstudier* (Lund: National Heritage Board).

Karsten, P. and Knarrström, B. (eds) (2003), *Skånska spår – arkeologi längs Västkustbanan. The Tågerup Excavations* (Lund: Riksantikvarieämbetet).

Keegan, J. (ed.) (1989), *The Times Atlas of the Second World War* (New York: Harper).

Knytlinge Saga = Bekker-Nielsen 1977.

Koch, E. (1998), *Neolithic Bog Pots from Zealand, Møn, Lolland and Falster* (København: Det Kongelige nordiske Oldskriftselskab).

Koch, J. and Roesdahl, E. (eds) (2005), *Boringholm. En østjysk træborg fra 1300-årene* (Højbjerg: Jysk Arkæologisk Selskab/Aarhus Universitetsforlag).

Kornerup, J. (1866), 'Gumløse Kirke i Skåne', *Aarbøger for Nordisk Oldkyndighed og Historie* 1866: 172ff.

Krogh, K.J. (1993), *Gåden om Kong Gorms Grav. Historien om Nordhøjen i Jelling* (København: Carlsbergfondet & Nationalmuseet).

Krogh, K.J. and Leth-Larsen, B. (2007), *Hedenskab og Kristent. Fundene fra den kongelige gravhøj i Jelling* (København: Carlsbergfondet & Nationalmuseet).

La Cour, V. (1961), *Næsholm* (København: Nationalmuseet).

Ladewig Petersen, E. (1980), *Fra standssamfund til rangsamfund 1500-1700. Dansk social historie 3* (København: Gyldendal).

Langberg, H. (1955), *Danmarks Bygningskultur. En historisk Oversigt I-II. Udgivet med Støtte af Grundejernes Hypothekforening i Anledning af Foreningens Jubilæum 18. Februar 1955* (København: Gyldendal; Nordisk Forlag).

Larsson, L. (1988), *Ett fångstsamhälle för 7000 år sedan. Boplatser och gravar i Skateholm* (Lund: Signum).

Liebgott, N.-K. (1989), *Dansk middelalderarkæologi* (København: Gad).

Lund, H. and Millech, K. (eds) (1963), *Danmarks bygningskunst. Fra Oldtid til Nutid* (København: Hirschsprung).

Lund, N. (1996), *Lið, leding og landeværn. Hær og samfund i Danmark i ældre middelalder* (Roskilde: Vikingeskibshallen).

Lund, N. (1998), *Harald Blåtands død og hans begravelse i Roskilde?* (Roskilde: Roskilde Museum).

Lund, N. (ed.) (2004), *Kristendommen i Danmark før 1050. Et symposium i Roskilde den 5.-7. februar 2003* (Roskilde: Roskilde Museum).

Lund, N. and Hørby, K. (1980), *Samfundet i vikingetid og middelalder 800-1500. Dansk socialhistorie 2* (København: Gyldendal).

Lund Hansen, U. et al. (1995), *Himlingeøje – Seeland – Europa. Ein Gräberfeld der jüngeren römischen Kaiserzeit auf Seeland. Seine Bedeutung und internationalen Beziehungen* (København: Det Kongelige Nordiske Oldskriftselskab).

Mackeprang, M. (1941), *Danmarks middelalderlige Døbefonte* (København: Selskabet til Udgivelse af Danske Mindesmærker/Høst).

Mackeprang, M. (1948), *Jydske Granitportaler* (København: Selskabet til Udgivelse af Danske Mindesmærker/Høst).

Madsen, P.K. (2003), 'Middelalderlige kirketagværker i Sydvest- og Sønderjylland – eksempler på alder og typer', *Aarbøger for nordisk Oldkyndighed og Historie* 2003: 7ff.

Mortensen, P. and Rasmussen, B.M. (eds) (1988), *Fra Stamme til Stat i Danmark. Jernalderens stammesamfund* (Højbjerg: Jysk Arkæologisk Selskab/Aarhus Universitetsforlag).

Müller-Wille, M. (1982), 'Königsgrab und Königsgrabkirche. Funde und Befunde im frühgeschichtlichen und mittelalterlichen Nordeuropa', *Berichte der römisch-germanischen Kommission* 63: 349ff.

Nielsen, I. (1987), *Bevar din arv. 1937 – Danmarks fortidsminder – 1987* (København: Gad/Skov- og Naturstyrelsen).

Nielsen, N., Skautrup, P. and Engelstoft, P. (eds) (1958-72), *J.P. Trap Danmark* (5th edn), 15 vols (København: Gad).

Nielsen, P.O. (2001), *Oldtiden i Danmark. Bondestenalderen* (København: Sesam).

Nørby, S. (2003), *Flådens sænkning 29. august 1943* (Odense: Region).

Nørlund, P. (1926), *Gyldne Altre. Jysk Metalkunst fra Valdemarstiden* (København: Selskabet til udgivelse af Danske Mindesmærker/Høst).

Norn, O. (1954), *Kronborgs bastioner. Et fortifikationshistorisk* (København: Schultz).

Olsen, O. (1960), 'Udgravningerne i Sct. Jørgensbjerg Kirke. Arkæologiske undersøgelser i murværk og gulv', *Aarbøger for nordisk Oldkyndighed og Historie* 1960: 1ff.

Olsen, O. (1978), *Christian IVs tugt- og børnehus* (Højbjerg: Wormianum).

Olsen, O., Schmidt, H. and Roesdahl, E. (1977), *Fyrkat. En jysk vikingeborg* vol. 1. *Borgen og bebyggelsen*; vol. 2 *Oldsagerne og gravpladsen* (København: Det kgl. nordiske Oldskriftselskab/Lynge).

Olsen, O. (ed.) (1988-), *Gyldendal og Politikens Danmarkshistorie*, 16 vols (København: Gyldendal & Politiken).

Olsen, O. and Crumlin-Pedersen, O. (1967), 'The Skuldelev Ships. (II). A Report on the Final Underwater Excavation in 1959 and the Savaging Operation in 1962', *Acta Archaeologica* 38: 73ff.

Olsen, R.A. (1996), *Borge i Danmark* (København: Fremad).

Olsson, M., Skansjö, S. and Sundberg, K. (eds) (2006), *Gods och bönder från hög-medeltid till nutid. Kontinuitet genem omvandling på Vittskövle och andra skånska gods* (Lund: Nordic Academic Press).

Opmålinger = Opmålinger. Årgangene 1906-1910. Udgivne af Foreningen af 3. december 1892 (København: Foreningen af 3. december 1892).

Pedersen, A. (1996), 'Søllested – nye oplysninger om et velkendt fund', *Aarbøger for nordisk Oldkyndighed og Historie* 1996: 37ff.

Petersen, E. Brinch (1974), 'Gravene ved Dragsholm. Fra jægere til bønder for 600 år siden', *Nationalmuseets Arbejdsmark* 1974: 112ff.

Petersen, H. (1888), *Vognfundene i Dejbjerg Præstegaardsmose ved Ringkjøbing 1881 og 1883. Bidrag til Oplysning om den førromerske Jernalder i Danmark* (Kjøbenhavn).

Pestell, T. and Ulmschneider, K. (eds) (2003), *Markets in Early Medieval Europe: Trading and 'Productive' Sites. 650-850* (Macclesfield: Windgather).

Pontoppidan, E. (1968-73 [1763-81]), *Den danske Atlas. Eller Konge-Riget Dannemark, med dets naturlige Egenskaber, Elementer, Indbyggere, Væxter, Dyr og andre Afødninger, dets gamle Tildragelser og nærværende Omstændigheder i alle Provintzer, Stæder, Kirker, Slotte og Herre-Gaarde. Forestillet ved en udførlig Lands-Beskrivelse, saa og oplyst med dertil for-færdigede Land-Kort. 1-7/8 [I-IX]* (København: Rosenkilde & Bagger).

Price, T.D., Knipper, C., Grupe, G. and Smrcka, V. (2004), 'Strontium Isotopes and Prehistoric Human Migration. The Bell Beaker Period in Central Europe', *European Journal of Archaeology* 7/1: 9ff.

Price, T.D., Ambrose, S.H., Bennike, P., Heinemeier, J., Noe-Nygaard, N.,

Brinch Petersen, E., Vang Petersen, P. and Richards, M.P. (2007), 'New Information on the Stone Age Graves at Dragsholm, Denmark', *Acta Archaeologica* 78: 193ff.

Radke, C. and Körber, W. (eds) (1984), *850 Jahre St.-Petri-Dom zu Schleswig. 1134-1984* (Schleswig: Ev.-Luth. Domgemeinde Schleswig/Schleswiger Druck- und Verlagshaus).

Randsborg, K. (1980), *The Viking Age in Denmark: The Formation of a State* (London & New York: Duckworth & St Martin's Press).

Randsborg, K. (1989), 'The Periods of Danish Antiquity', *Acta Archaeologica* 60: 187ff.

Randsborg, K. (1990), *The First Millennium AD in Europe and the Mediterranean: An Archaeological Essay* (Cambridge: Cambridge University Press).

Randsborg, K. (1992), 'Antiquity and Archaeology in "Bourgeois" Scandinavia 1750-1800', *Acta Archaeologica* 63: 209ff.

Randsborg, K. (1993), 'Kivik. Archaeology and Iconography', *Acta Archaeologica* 64: 1ff.

Randsborg, K. (1994), 'Ole Worm. An Essay on the Modernization of Antiquity', *Acta Archaeologica* 65: 135ff.

Randsborg, K. (1995), *Hjortspring. Warfare & Sacrifice in Early Europe* (Aarhus: Aarhus University Press).

Randsborg, K. (1998), 'Plundered Bronze Age Graves', *Acta Archaeologica* 69: 20ff.

Randsborg, K. (2003), 'Bastrup – Europe. A Massive Danish *Donjon* from 1100', *Acta Archaeologica* 74: 65ff.

Randsborg, K. (2004), 'Inigo Jones & Christian IV. Archaeological Encounters in Architecture', *Acta Archaeologica* 75:1.

Randsborg, K. (2008), 'Kings' Jelling. Gorm & Thyra's Palace – Harald's Monument & Grave – Svend's Cathedral', *Acta Archaeologica* 79: 1ff.

Randsborg, K. & Kjeld Christensen. (2006), 'Bronze Age Oak-Coffin Graves. Archaeology & Dendro-Dating', *Acta Archaeologica* 77.

Renfrew, C. and Bahn, P. (1991 & later), *Archaeology: Theories, Methods and Practice* (London: Thames & Hudson).

Roesdahl, E. (ed.) (2003), *Bolig og familie i Danmarks middelalder* (Højbjerg: Jysk Arkæologisk Selskab).

Roslund, M. (2001), *Gäster i huset. Kulturell överföring mellan slaver och skandinaver 900 till 1300* (Lund: Vetenskapssocieteten i Lund).

Ræder Knudsen, L. (2007), 'Høvding og præst?', *Skalk* 6: 3ff.

van der Sanden, W. (1996), *Udødeliggjorte i mosen. Historierne om de nordvesteuropæiske moselig* (Assen: Drents Museum/Batavian Lion).

Saxo = P. Zeeberg (ed.) (2000), *Saxos Danmarkshistorie* (København: Det Danske Sprog- og Litteraturselskab/Gad).

Scarre, C. (ed.) (2005), *The Human Past: World Prehistory and the Development of Human Societies* (London: Thames & Hudson).

Schmidt, C.M. and Johannsen, H. (1981), *Danmarks Arkitektur. Kirkens huse* (København: Gyldendal).

Schück, A. (ed.) (1938), *Befolkning under medeltiden* (Stockholm/Oslo/København: Bonnier/Aschehoug/Schultz).

Sherratt, A. (ed.) (1980), *The Cambridge Encyclopaedia of Archaeology* (Cambridge: Cambridge University Press).

Skov, H. (1994), *Hustyper i vikingetid og tidlig middelalder. Udviklingen af hus-*

Bibliography

typerne i det gammeldanske område fra ca. 800-1200 (Højbjerg: Hikuin): 139ff.

Smith, A.J. (2007), 'Century-Scale Holocene Processes as a Source of Natural Selection Pressure in Human Evolution: Holocene Climate and the Human Genome Project', *The Holocene* 17/5: 689ff.

Sørensen, A.C. (2001), *Ladby: A Danish Ship-Grave from the Viking Age* (Roskilde: The Viking Ship Museum in Roskilde).

Skre, D. (2007), *Kaupang in Skiringssal* (Aarhus: Aarhus University Press).

Storck, H. (ed.) (1911), *Tegninger af ældre nordisk Architektur V:3* (København: Hagerup).

Storck, H. (1915), *Tegninger af ældre nordisk Architektur VI:1* (København: Hagerup).

Svart Kristiansen, M. (ed.) (2005), *Tårnby. Gård og landsby gennem 1000 år* (Højbjerg: Jysk Arkæologisk Selskab/Aarhus Universitetsforlag).

Svensmark, H. (2007), 'Cosmoclimatology: a New Theory Emerges', *Astronomy & Geophysics* 48/1: 118ff.

Svensmark, H., Pepke Pedersen, J.O., Marsh, N., Enghoff, M. and Uggerhøj, U. (2007), 'Experimental Evidence for the role of Ions in Particle Nucleation under Atmospheric Conditions', *Proceedings of the Royal Society A: Mathematical, Physical and Engineering Sciences* 463: 385ff.

Thurah, L. de. (1746-49), *Den Danske VITRUVIUS Indeholder Grundtegninger, Opstalter, og Giennemsnitter af de merkværdigste Bygninger i Kongeriget Dannemark, samt de Kongelige Tydske Provintzer, Tilligemed en kort Beskrivelse over hver Bygning i sær. Deelt i Tvende Deele. Den Første Handler om de fornemmeste Bygninger, som findes i den kongel. Hoved-Residentz- og frie Riigs-Stad Kiøbenhavn, saavel kongelige, offentlige, som en Deel Privat-Bygninger Den Anden Indeholder alle Kongelige Slotte, saavelsom en Deel andre merkværdige Bygninger i Kongeriget Dannemark saavelsom i de Kongelige Tydske Provintzer. I-II.* [Text also in French and German] (København: Berling).

Ulriksen, J. (1994), 'Danish Sites and Settlements with a Maritime Context: AD 200-1200', *Antiquity* 68: 797ff.

Ulsig, E. (1991), 'Pest og befolkningsnedgang i Danmark i det 14. århundrede', *Historisk Tidsskrift* Række 6, Bind 5: 21ff.

Wamers, E. (1994), 'König im Grenzland: Neue Analyse des Bootkammergrabes vom Haiðaby', *Acta Archaeologica* 65: 1ff. (esp. 32ff.).

Wanscher, V. (1939), *Kronborgs Historie* (København: Fischer).

Westholm, G. (2007), *Visby. 1361. Invasionen* (Stockholm: Prisma).

Wienberg, J. (1993), *Den gotiske labyrint. Middelalderen og kirkerne i Danmark* (Stockholm: Almqvist & Wiksell).

Wimmer, L.F.A. (1893-1908), *De danske Runemindesmærker. Undersøgte og tolkede. I-IV* (København: Gyldendal).

Worm, O. (1643-51), *Danicorum Monumentorum Libri Sex. E spissis antiquitatum tenebris et in Dania ac Norvegia extantibus ruderibus eruti. & Additamenta ad Monumenta Danica* (Hafniae: Moltke).

Worm, O. (1655), *Museum Wormianum. Seu historia rerum rariorum, tam naturalium, quam artificialium, tam domesticarum, quam exoticarum, quæ Hafniæ Danorum in ædibus authoris servantur. Variis et accuratis iconibus illustrata / adornata* (Amstelodami).

Index of Places

Index of Personal Names

CPSIA information can be obtained
at www.ICGtesting.com
Printed in the USA
LVOW13s2019310718

585496LV00006B/7/P